I0008420

Harnessing the Power of Cross-Platform Development

Innovative Techniques in Python and C# for Modern Software Engineering

THOMPSON CARTER

All rights reserved

No part of this book may be reproduced, distributed, or transmitted in any form or by any means without the prior written permission of the publisher, except in the case of brief quotations embodied in critical reviews and certain other noncommercial uses permitted by right law.

Table of Content

TABLE OF CONTENTS

Introduction

In the ever-evolving world of software development, building applications that seamlessly run across multiple platforms has become an essential goal for many developers. The challenge of creating applications that work across **Windows, macOS, Linux, and mobile platforms** like **Android** and **iOS** has led to the rise of **cross-platform development**. This approach not only saves time and resources but also ensures that your application reaches a broader audience without compromising performance or user experience.

"Harnessing the Power of Cross-Platform Development" is your comprehensive guide to understanding and mastering the art of developing robust, scalable, and efficient cross-platform applications using two of the most powerful programming languages today: **Python** and **C#**.

Why Cross-Platform Development?

The rise of **mobile computing, cloud technologies**, and the increasing need for **global accessibility** has made cross-platform development an essential skill for modern software engineers. Gone are the days when developers could focus on just one operating system or platform. Today's applications need to work seamlessly across a diverse range of devices, operating systems, and environments. As users expect a consistent experience, businesses are increasingly relying on cross-platform solutions to reduce development time and costs, while also providing a universal product for their users.

This book provides you with the **knowledge and tools** to successfully build cross-platform applications using **Python and C#**. Whether you are a beginner or an experienced developer, you will find this book a valuable resource for developing high-quality applications across multiple platforms.

What You Will Learn

This book is designed to help you navigate the entire cross-platform development process, from **choosing the right tech stack** to **deployment and scaling**. It covers both high-level strategies and hands-on coding examples, ensuring that you can build practical, real-world applications. Here's an overview of what you'll learn:

Understanding the Basics of Cross-Platform Development

You'll begin by understanding the core principles of cross-platform development. You'll learn about the different types of cross-platform approaches, from hybrid frameworks to fully native development, and how languages like Python and C# fit into the mix. This foundation will help you decide which framework is best suited for your project and how to approach cross-platform development with the right mindset.

Exploring Python and C# for Cross-Platform Applications

Python and C# are two of the most widely used programming languages for cross-platform development. In this book, we dive deep into the strengths and capabilities of each language and how they can be leveraged for building efficient cross-platform solutions.

- **Python**: Known for its versatility, Python is widely used in backend development, machine learning, and web development. You'll learn how to use **Python frameworks** like **Tkinter**, **PyQt**, **Kivy**, and **Flask** to build powerful applications that work seamlessly across platforms.

- **C#**: A primary language for **Microsoft technologies**, C# is a robust, high-performance language used to build everything from **enterprise applications** to **mobile apps**. You'll explore **.NET MAUI**, **Xamarin**, and **Blazor**, and see how these tools can help you create native applications for mobile, desktop, and web platforms.

Building Practical Cross-Platform Applications

With a strong foundation in both Python and C#, we'll guide you through building real-world cross-platform applications. From **command-line tools** to **GUI apps** and **web services**, you will gain hands-on experience in writing code that runs smoothly on multiple platforms.

- Learn how to use **multi-threading** and **asynchronous programming** to improve performance.
- Develop a solid understanding of **testing** and **debugging** tools and techniques to ensure your applications run efficiently across various environments.
- Discover best practices for **structuring your project** and organizing your code for easy maintainability and scalability.

Embracing Emerging Technologies

As we move toward the future, the development landscape continues to change with the introduction of new frameworks, tools, and technologies. This book doesn't just cover today's cross-platform approaches but also delves into **emerging trends** that will shape the future of application development, including **AI and machine learning** integration, **WebAssembly**, and **Progressive Web Apps (PWAs)**.

Real-World Case Studies

You'll also find **real-world case studies** from successful companies that have effectively used cross-platform tools to build scalable, maintainable applications. Learn from the experiences of industry leaders like **Spotify**, **Dropbox**, and **Microsoft Visual Studio Code**, and gain insights into how they overcame common challenges in cross-platform development.

Who This Book Is For

This book is ideal for anyone interested in **building cross-platform applications**. Whether you are a novice developer starting your journey or an experienced professional looking to expand your skill set, this book provides clear, actionable insights to help you succeed in your projects.

- **Beginners** will find this book approachable, as it breaks down complex concepts into digestible sections, with plenty of practical examples and easy-to-understand explanations.
- **Experienced developers** will appreciate the depth of content that explores advanced techniques in cross-platform development, debugging, testing, and performance optimization.

If you're looking to gain expertise in developing **mobile apps**, **desktop applications**, or **web apps** that run across multiple platforms, this book will give you all the tools and knowledge you need to build high-quality software that performs well on all target environments.

How This Book Is Structured

The chapters of this book are organized to provide a gradual learning experience. You'll start with foundational concepts, build your skills step-by-step, and work through practical examples as you progress.

1. **Part 1: Introduction to Cross-Platform Development** – Understand the core principles and how Python and C# can be used for cross-platform development.

2. **Part 2: Python and C# – A Powerful Combination** – Dive into both Python and C# development for cross-platform apps.

3. **Part 3: Building Cross-Platform Applications** – Learn the technical skills necessary to develop cross-platform CLI, GUI, and web applications.

4. **Part 4: Cross-Platform Systems & Frameworks** – Gain expertise in packaging, frameworks, and performance considerations for cross-platform development.

5. **Part 5: Advanced Techniques and Performance Optimization** – Learn how to profile, optimize, and debug your cross-platform applications to improve performance.

6. **Part 6: Real-World Applications & Future Trends** – Explore real-world case studies and the future of cross-platform development, including emerging technologies like AI and PWAs.

Conclusion

By the end of this book, you will have a solid understanding of **how to choose the right tools and frameworks** for cross-platform development, as well as the skills to build, optimize, and maintain applications that run seamlessly across multiple platforms. Whether you're building a **web application**, a **desktop app**, or a **mobile solution**, this book will equip you with the knowledge to develop software that performs efficiently, looks great, and provides a consistent user experience across all platforms.

Let's dive in and start your journey to becoming a cross-platform development expert!

PART 1

INTRODUCTION TO CROSS-PLATFORM DEVELOPMENT

CHAPTER 1

UNDERSTANDING CROSS-PLATFORM DEVELOPMENT

Cross-platform development has transformed the way software is built and deployed. Instead of developing separate applications for each operating system (Windows, macOS, Linux) or device type (desktop, mobile, web), developers can now write a single codebase that runs seamlessly across multiple platforms. This chapter introduces the core concepts, benefits, and challenges of cross-platform development while exploring how **Python** and **C#** play a crucial role in modern software engineering.

What is Cross-Platform Development?

Cross-platform development refers to the practice of writing software that can run on multiple operating systems and hardware environments with little to no modification. Instead of writing separate versions of an application for Windows, macOS, and Linux (or Android and iOS), developers use cross-platform frameworks, libraries, and programming languages to streamline the process.

There are **three main approaches** to cross-platform development:

1. **Native Cross-Platform Development** – Uses shared business logic but platform-specific UI components. Example: **.NET MAUI, Xamarin**
2. **Hybrid Development** – Uses web technologies (HTML, CSS, JavaScript) wrapped in a native container. Example: **Electron, React Native**
3. **Interpreted or Virtual Machine-Based** – Uses languages that run in a cross-platform runtime. Example: **Python, Java, .NET Core**

By leveraging the right tools, developers can build applications that maintain high performance, native-like user experience, and broad accessibility.

Advantages & Challenges of Cross-Platform Development

Advantages

1. **Code Reusability** – Developers write a single codebase that runs across multiple platforms, reducing development time and effort.

2. **Faster Development & Deployment** – Changes and updates can be pushed to all platforms simultaneously.

3. **Cost-Effective** – Businesses save on development, testing, and maintenance costs.

4. **Wider Market Reach** – Applications can reach users regardless of their operating system or device.

5. **Consistent User Experience** – UI/UX remains uniform across platforms, improving usability.

Challenges

1. **Performance Trade-offs** – Some cross-platform frameworks can be slower than native development.

2. **Limited Access to Native Features** – Some platform-specific APIs may require additional workarounds.

3. **Compatibility Issues** – Not all libraries and dependencies work seamlessly across platforms.

4. **UI/UX Differences** – Different platforms have their own design guidelines (e.g., Material Design for Android, Human Interface Guidelines for macOS).

5. **Security Considerations** – Cross-platform applications may require additional security measures to handle platform-specific vulnerabilities.

Despite these challenges, advancements in **.NET Core, .NET MAUI, Python, and modern frameworks** have made cross-platform development more efficient than ever.

Why Python and C# for Cross-Platform Development?

Both **Python** and **C#** are powerful languages for cross-platform development, but they serve different roles:

Python: The Versatile Powerhouse

Python is widely known for its simplicity and flexibility, making it an excellent choice for cross-platform applications. Some key reasons why Python is used:

- **Interpreted Language** – Runs on multiple OS without recompilation.
- **Rich Ecosystem** – Supports GUI development (**Tkinter, PyQt, Kivy**), web frameworks (**Django, Flask**), and mobile development (**BeeWare, Kivy**).

- **Strong Community Support** – One of the largest and most active programming communities.
- **Great for Scripting & Automation** – Ideal for backend services, CLI tools, and automation scripts.

Popular Cross-Platform Apps Built with Python:

- **Dropbox** (Uses Python for backend services)
- **YouTube** (Initially built with Python)
- **Instagram** (Uses Django, a Python web framework)
- **Spotify** (Relies on Python for data analysis and backend processing)

C#: The Enterprise-Ready Workhorse

C# is a high-performance, statically typed language developed by Microsoft, optimized for cross-platform development through **.NET Core** and **.NET MAUI**. Some key advantages:

- **Compiled Language** – Faster than interpreted languages like Python.
- **.NET Core & .NET MAUI** – Enables cross-platform desktop, mobile, and cloud application development.
- **Rich UI Frameworks** – Supports **WPF, Xamarin, Avalonia, and Blazor** for GUI applications.

- **Seamless Integration with Microsoft Ecosystem** – Ideal for enterprise applications.

Popular Cross-Platform Apps Built with C#:

- **Microsoft Teams** (Built with C# and .NET Core)
- **Unity Engine** (Uses C# for game development)
- **Visual Studio Code** (Developed using Electron, with some C# components)
- **Skype** (Uses C# for desktop and backend services)

Examples of Real-World Cross-Platform Applications

Here are some widely used **cross-platform applications** that showcase the power of cross-platform development:

Application	Technology Used	Platforms Supported
Visual Studio Code	Electron (JavaScript), C#	Windows, macOS, Linux
Slack	Electron (JavaScript), Python	Windows, macOS, Linux, Web

Application	Technology Used	Platforms Supported
Microsoft Teams	.NET Core (C#), Angular	Windows, macOS, Web, Mobile
Spotify	Python, C++	Windows, macOS, Linux, Web
Unity Game Engine	C#	Windows, macOS, Android, iOS, Web
Dropbox	Python, Go	Windows, macOS, Linux
Blender	Python, C++	Windows, macOS, Linux

Each of these applications demonstrates how different languages, frameworks, and tools can be used to build powerful **multi-platform software.**

Summary

- **Cross-platform development** allows developers to write code once and deploy it across multiple operating systems and devices.

- **Python and C#** are two of the best languages for cross-platform development due to their **robust ecosystems, performance, and scalability**.
- **Real-world applications like Spotify, Dropbox, Unity, and Visual Studio Code** demonstrate the power of cross-platform frameworks.
- While **cross-platform development offers significant benefits**, developers must consider **performance trade-offs, UI/UX consistency, and security concerns**.

What's Next?

In the next chapter, we'll dive deeper into the **core principles of cross-platform development**, discussing key concepts like **frameworks, SDKs, APIs, and best practices for designing maintainable cross-platform applications**.

CHAPTER 2

CORE PRINCIPLES OF CROSS-PLATFORM DEVELOPMENT

Cross-platform development is built on foundational principles that allow developers to **write code once and run it anywhere** while ensuring performance and usability across different platforms. This chapter will explore these principles, focusing on **code reusability, platform independence, and optimization techniques**, as well as the role of **frameworks, SDKs, and APIs** in achieving seamless cross-platform compatibility.

Writing Code Once, Running It Anywhere

One of the biggest advantages of cross-platform development is the ability to **reuse a single codebase** across multiple operating systems, minimizing development effort and maintenance.

How It Works

Developers leverage programming languages, frameworks, and tools that abstract platform-specific details. Instead of writing separate applications for Windows, macOS, Linux, Android, and iOS, they use:

- **Interpreted languages (e.g., Python)** that run within an interpreter available across platforms.
- **Cross-platform frameworks (e.g., .NET Core, .NET MAUI, Qt, Electron, Kivy)** that provide a unified way to develop for multiple environments.
- **Web-based technologies (e.g., Progressive Web Apps, Blazor, React Native)** that run in a browser-like container across different devices.

Key Benefits

Faster Development – Reduces duplication of work.
Easier Maintenance – Bug fixes and updates apply to all platforms   simultaneously.
Cost-Efficient – Businesses save money by avoiding platform-specific teams.

Examples of "Write Once, Run Anywhere" Technologies

Technology	Language	Platforms Supported
.NET Core	C#	Windows, macOS, Linux
Python	Python	Windows, macOS, Linux, Web
Kivy	Python	Windows, macOS, Linux, Android, iOS
Electron	JavaScript	Windows, macOS, Linux
Qt	C++	Windows, macOS, Linux, Android, iOS
React Native	JavaScript	iOS, Android

Despite the advantages, **platform-specific challenges** still exist, such as UI differences and performance trade-offs.

Platform Independence vs. Native Optimization

While cross-platform development emphasizes code reusability, it must also balance **platform independence** and **native performance**.

1. Platform Independence

- The goal is to create applications that behave **consistently** across different environments.
- **Abstracts away platform-specific code** to focus on business logic.
- Typically **achieved through frameworks like .NET MAUI, Qt, and Kivy.**
- **Best for:** Web applications, desktop apps that don't require deep OS-level integration.

Example: **Dropbox**

Dropbox's desktop application is written in Python and works seamlessly across Windows, macOS, and Linux **without modification**.

2. Native Optimization

- Some applications require **platform-specific enhancements** to achieve maximum performance and user experience.
- UI components, system calls, and performance tuning **must align with each platform's best practices**.
- Achieved through **conditional compilation, platform-specific libraries, and native APIs**.
- **Best for:** Performance-intensive applications like **video editors, 3D rendering tools, and real-time gaming apps**.

36

Example: **Microsoft** **Teams**

Built using **Electron**, but optimized for Windows and macOS with **native code for notifications, performance, and hardware acceleration**.

Choosing the Right Approach

Factor	Platform Independence	Native Optimization
Performance	Good, but may have overhead	Excellent, optimized for each OS
Development Speed	Faster, single codebase	Slower, requires per-platform coding
Maintenance	Easier, updates apply to all platforms	Harder, requires separate updates
Best For	Business apps, web-based solutions, general utilities	High-performance apps, games, hardware-intensive applications

Many developers use **hybrid approaches** where a core application remains platform-independent, but certain modules are **natively optimized**.

Understanding Frameworks, SDKs, and APIs

Cross-platform development relies on **frameworks, Software Development Kits (SDKs), and Application Programming Interfaces (APIs)** to simplify the process.

1. Frameworks

A **framework** provides a structured way to build applications, offering pre-built components, libraries, and development guidelines.

Framework	Language	Platforms Supported	Use Case
.NET MAUI	C#	Windows, macOS, Android, iOS	GUI applications
Electron	JavaScript	Windows, macOS, Linux	Web-based desktop apps
Kivy	Python	Windows, macOS, Linux, Android, iOS	GUI applications

Framework	Language	Platforms Supported	Use Case
Flutter	Dart	Android, iOS, Web, macOS, Windows	Mobile & Web apps

Example: Spotify Desktop is built with a combination of **C++, Python, and Electron** for cross-platform capability.

---

2. SDKs (Software Development Kits)

An **SDK** is a collection of tools, libraries, and documentation designed to help developers build applications for a specific platform.

Popular SDKs for Cross-Platform Development:

SDK	Purpose	Supported Platforms
.NET SDK	Developing .NET applications	Windows, macOS, Linux
Android SDK	Mobile app development	Android

39

SDK	Purpose	Supported Platforms
iOS SDK	Mobile app development	iOS
Qt SDK	GUI and cross-platform apps	Windows, macOS, Linux
Unity SDK	Game development	Windows, macOS, Android, iOS

Example: Xamarin SDK (now part of .NET MAUI) allows **C# developers** to build mobile apps for **Android and iOS** using a shared codebase.

3. APIs (Application Programming Interfaces)

APIs act as **bridges** between your application and platform-specific features, enabling interaction with the OS, hardware, and other services.

Types of APIs Used in Cross-Platform Development:

1. **Web APIs** – Allow applications to communicate over the internet (e.g., **RESTful APIs, GraphQL**).

2. **Native OS APIs** – Provide access to system-level features like file handling, networking, and hardware.

3. **Third-Party APIs** – Enable integration with external services (e.g., **Google Maps API, Stripe API for payments**).

Example: Google Drive API lets applications access Google Drive storage across different platforms.

Summary

- **Writing code once and running it anywhere** is the foundation of cross-platform development, achieved through frameworks like **.NET MAUI, Python, and Electron**.

- Developers must balance **platform independence** and **native optimization** depending on performance and UX needs.

- **Frameworks (e.g., Qt, Flutter, Kivy)** provide structured tools for development.

- **SDKs** equip developers with platform-specific tools.

- **APIs** enable communication between applications and platform-specific features.

What's Next?

In the next chapter, we will explore **how to set up a cross-platform development environment**, covering **essential tools, configurations, and best practices** to ensure smooth development across Windows, macOS, and Linux.

CHAPTER 3

SETTING UP YOUR DEVELOPMENT ENVIRONMENT

A well-configured development environment is essential for efficient and seamless **cross-platform application development**. This chapter provides a step-by-step guide to setting up **Python and C#**, the best development tools available, how to manage dependencies using **virtual environments and package managers**, and best practices for maintaining cross-platform projects.

1. Installing Python and C#

Python and C# require different setups depending on your operating system. Below is a guide for **Windows, macOS, and Linux**.

Installing Python

Python is available on all major operating systems, and installing it is straightforward.

43

Windows

1. Download the latest Python version from the official Python website.
2. Run the installer and check **"Add Python to PATH"** before clicking "Install."
3. Verify the installation by opening **Command Prompt** and running:

```sh
python --version
```

macOS

1. Install Python via **Homebrew**:

```sh
brew install python
```

2. Verify the installation:

```sh
python3 --version
```

Linux (Ubuntu/Debian)

1. Install Python using `apt`:

```sh
sh
```

```sh
sudo apt update && sudo apt install python3
python3-pip -y
```

2. Check the installation:

```sh
sh
```

```sh
python3 --version
```

Installing C# and .NET SDK

C# requires the **.NET SDK**, which includes everything needed to develop and run .NET applications.

Windows

1. Download and install the latest **.NET SDK** from the official Microsoft website.
2. Verify the installation:

```sh
sh
```

```sh
dotnet --version
```

macOS

1. Install the .NET SDK using Homebrew:

45

```sh
```

```sh
brew install dotnet
```

2. Check the installation:

```sh
```

```sh
dotnet --version
```

Linux (Ubuntu/Debian)

1. Install the .NET SDK using:

```sh
```

```sh
sudo apt update
sudo apt install dotnet-sdk-7.0
```

2. Verify the installation:

```sh
```

```sh
dotnet --version
```

2. Essential Tools for Cross-Platform Development

Several tools enhance the development experience when working with Python and C#. Below are some of the best IDEs and editors for cross-platform development.

1. Integrated Development Environments (IDEs)

Tool	Best For	Supported Languages	Platforms
Visual Studio Code	Lightweight development	Python, C#	Windows, macOS, Linux
Visual Studio	Full-fledged C# development	C#, Python	Windows, macOS
JetBrains Rider	Advanced .NET development	C#	Windows, macOS, Linux
PyCharm	Python development	Python	Windows, macOS, Linux
Eclipse with PyDev	Open-source Python IDE	Python	Windows, macOS, Linux

Recommended Choice:

- **Visual Studio Code** – Ideal for both **Python and C#**, lightweight, and cross-platform.
- **JetBrains Rider** – Best for **.NET developers** who need a powerful C# IDE.
- **PyCharm** – Great for **Python developers** working on complex projects.

2. Command-Line Interfaces & Terminals

Tool	Best For	Platforms
Windows Terminal	PowerShell, WSL, and CMD	Windows
iTerm2	Improved terminal for developers	macOS
GNOME Terminal	Default for Linux	Linux

A powerful terminal setup helps in running scripts, managing dependencies, and debugging applications efficiently.

3. Configuring Virtual Environments & Package Managers

Virtual environments and package managers help manage dependencies and keep projects isolated.

Python: Virtual Environments & Pip

Python projects should be managed using **virtual environments**, which allow dependencies to be installed in a self-contained directory instead of system-wide.

Setting Up a Virtual Environment

1. Navigate to your project folder and create a virtual environment:

   ```sh
   python -m venv venv
   ```

2. Activate the virtual environment:
   o **Windows:**

      ```sh
      venv\Scripts\activate
      ```

49

- o **macOS/Linux:**

```sh
source venv/bin/activate
```

3. Install dependencies:

```sh
pip install requests flask
```

4. Save dependencies for easy setup in other environments:

```sh
pip freeze > requirements.txt
```

5. Deactivate the virtual environment:

```sh
deactivate
```

Python Package Managers

- **pip** – Default package manager for Python.
- **pipenv** – Combines virtual environments and dependency management.
- **poetry** – Modern dependency manager for Python projects.

50

C#: NuGet and Dependency Management

C# projects use **NuGet**, a package manager designed for .NET applications.

Using NuGet in a .NET Project

1. Create a new .NET project:

    ```sh
    dotnet new console -n MyApp
    ```

2. Navigate to the project directory:

    ```sh
    cd MyApp
    ```

3. Add a NuGet package (e.g., JSON serialization library):

    ```sh
    dotnet add package Newtonsoft.Json
    ```

4. Restore dependencies:

    ```sh
    ```

51

```
dotnet restore
```

Other C# Package Managers

- **Paket** – Alternative to NuGet with better dependency management.
- **Chocolatey** – Windows package manager useful for setting up development tools.

---

4. Best Practices for Maintaining Cross-Platform Projects

Keeping a cross-platform project maintainable requires following best practices in **code organization, version control, and testing**.

1. Project Structure

Organizing code properly helps in scaling and maintaining cross-platform applications.

Recommended Project Structure for a Python + C# Project

bash

```
/MyCrossPlatformApp
|— /src
|    |— /python_code
|    |    ├— main.py
|    |    ├— utils.py
|    |— /csharp_code
|    |    ├— Program.cs
|    |    ├— Utilities.cs
|— /tests
|    |— /python_tests
|    |— /csharp_tests
|— requirements.txt
|— MyCrossPlatformApp.sln
|— README.md
```

2. Version Control (Git)

Use Git for version control to track changes and collaborate efficiently.

Basic Git Workflow

sh

```
git init
git add .
git commit -m "Initial commit"
git branch -M main
git remote add origin <repo-url>
git push -u origin main
```

3. Cross-Platform Testing

- Use **unit testing frameworks**:
    - **Python:** pytest, unittest
    - **C#:** xUnit, NUnit
- Automate tests with **GitHub Actions, Azure DevOps, or Jenkins**.

Summary

- **Python and C# installations** vary across Windows, macOS, and Linux.
- **Essential tools like Visual Studio, JetBrains Rider, and PyCharm** improve development productivity.
- **Virtual environments (Python) and NuGet (C#)** help manage dependencies efficiently.
- **Following best practices in code organization, version control, and testing** ensures maintainability.

What's Next?

In the next chapter, we will explore **building Python and C# applications for different platforms**, covering desktop, web, and mobile development techniques!

PART 2

INTRODUCTION TO CROSS-PLATFORM DEVELOPMENT

CHAPTER 4

PYTHON FOR CROSS-PLATFORM APPLICATIONS

Python is one of the most versatile programming languages, making it an excellent choice for **cross-platform development**. Its flexibility allows developers to build applications that run seamlessly across **Windows, macOS, and Linux**. This chapter explores **Python's strengths in cross-platform projects**, the **best libraries for GUI development**, and how to **package Python applications for different operating systems**.

---

1. Python's Versatility in Cross-Platform Projects

Python's ability to run on multiple platforms without modification makes it a go-to language for **cross-platform application development**. Here's why:

Key Features That Make Python Ideal for Cross-Platform Development

Interpreted Language – Python scripts run without the need for recompilation across platforms.

Broad Library Support – Extensive built-in and third-party libraries simplify cross-platform development.

Multi-Paradigm – Supports object-oriented, functional, and procedural programming styles.

Rich GUI Development Options – Several frameworks (e.g., Tkinter, PyQt, Kivy) allow for easy user interface design.

Strong Community & Open Source – Supported by a large developer community with thousands of libraries available.

Types of Cross-Platform Applications You Can Build with Python

Application Type	Python Libraries/Tools
Desktop Applications	Tkinter, PyQt, Kivy
Web Applications	Django, Flask, FastAPI
Mobile Applications	Kivy, BeeWare (Toga)
Command-Line Tools	Argparse, Click, Typer

Application Type	Python Libraries/Tools
Data Science & AI	NumPy, Pandas, TensorFlow, Scikit-learn

Example: Dropbox uses Python for its backend services and desktop client.

---

2. Libraries for GUI Development in Python

Python provides several **cross-platform GUI frameworks** that allow developers to create desktop applications with **native-looking interfaces**.

1. Tkinter (Built-in GUI Library)

Best for: Simple desktop applications, beginners learning GUI   programming.
Pros:
Comes   pre-installed   with   Python.
Lightweight   and   easy   to   learn.
Works across **Windows, macOS, and Linux.**

Cons:

Limited UI customization.
Not suitable for complex applications.

Example: Creating a Simple Tkinter Window

```python

import tkinter as tk

root = tk.Tk()
root.title("Cross-Platform App")
root.geometry("300x200")

label = tk.Label(root, text="Hello, Python GUI!")
label.pack()

root.mainloop()
```

2. PyQt (Powerful GUI Framework Based on Qt)

Best for: High-performance desktop applications with modern UI.

Pros:

Feature-rich and highly customizable.
Runs on **Windows, macOS, and Linux**.

Provides built-in support for **multi-threading and database access**.

Cons:

Requires a commercial license for proprietary apps. Steeper learning curve compared to Tkinter.

Example: Simple PyQt5 App

```python
python

from PyQt5.QtWidgets import QApplication,
QLabel, QWidget
import sys

app = QApplication(sys.argv)
window = QWidget()
window.setWindowTitle("PyQt Cross-Platform App")
window.setGeometry(100, 100, 300, 200)

label = QLabel("Hello from PyQt!", window)
label.move(100, 90)

window.show()
sys.exit(app.exec_())
```

3. Kivy (Best for Mobile & Touch-Based Apps)

Best for: Mobile and touchscreen applications that need cross-platform support.

Pros:

Supports **Android, iOS, Windows, macOS, and Linux**. Works well with touch gestures. Highly customizable and GPU-accelerated.

Cons:

UI components differ from native elements, so styling takes more effort.

Requires additional setup for mobile deployment.

Example: Simple Kivy App

```python
from kivy.app import App
from kivy.uix.label import Label

class MyApp(App):
    def build(self):
        return Label(text="Hello, Kivy!")

MyApp().run()
```

When to Use Each Framework

Framework	Best For	Platforms
Tkinter	Simple GUI apps	Windows, macOS, Linux
PyQt	Advanced desktop applications	Windows, macOS, Linux
Kivy	Mobile & touchscreen apps	Windows, macOS, Linux, Android, iOS

3. Packaging Python Applications for Windows, macOS, and Linux

Once an application is developed, it needs to be **packaged** so users can run it **without installing Python separately**.

1. Packaging for Windows using PyInstaller

PyInstaller is the most popular tool for converting Python scripts into standalone executables.

Installing PyInstaller

sh

```
pip install pyinstaller
```

Creating a Standalone EXE

sh

```
pyinstaller --onefile --windowed myapp.py
```

Flags Explained:

- `--onefile`: Packages everything into a single executable.
- `--windowed`: Hides the console window (useful for GUI apps).

Final Output: The executable file will be located in the `dist/` directory.

---

2. Packaging for macOS using PyInstaller

On macOS, PyInstaller can also generate a **.app bundle**.

Building a macOS App

sh

```
pyinstaller    --onefile    --windowed    --name
"MyMacApp" myapp.py
```

The generated `.app` file will be inside the `dist/` directory.

Note: On macOS, you may need to sign and notarize your app to avoid security warnings.

---

3. Packaging for Linux

Linux users can also use **PyInstaller** to generate executable binaries.

Creating a Linux Executable

```sh

pyinstaller --onefile myapp.py
```

The final executable will be in `dist/`, and users can **run it without needing Python installed**.

Additional Options for Packaging

Tool	Best For	Platforms
PyInstaller	Standalone executables	Windows, macOS, Linux
cx_Freeze	Python-to-executable conversion	Windows, macOS, Linux

64

Tool	Best For	Platforms
PyOxidizer	Modern packaging with better performance	Windows, macOS, Linux

Summary

- **Python is a powerful choice for cross-platform development**, supporting applications across **Windows, macOS, Linux, and even mobile platforms**.
- **Tkinter, PyQt, and Kivy** are the most popular frameworks for **GUI development**.
- **PyInstaller** is the easiest way to package Python applications into **standalone executables**.
- **Each platform (Windows, macOS, Linux) has specific requirements for packaging and distribution.**

What's Next?

In the next chapter, we'll dive into **C# for cross-platform development**, exploring how **.NET Core, .NET MAUI, and Avalonia** enable cross-platform applications with **native performance**.

CHAPTER 5

C# FOR CROSS-PLATFORM DEVELOPMENT

C# has evolved into a **powerful language for cross-platform development**, thanks to advancements in **.NET Core, .NET MAUI, Blazor, Xamarin, and Avalonia**. Unlike earlier versions of .NET, which were primarily Windows-centric, modern **.NET (previously .NET Core)** enables developers to build applications that run seamlessly on **Windows, macOS, Linux, Android, and iOS**.

In this chapter, we'll explore **.NET Core and .NET MAUI**, popular cross-platform frameworks, and key differences between **Windows and Linux/macOS development**.

---

1. The Role of .NET Core & .NET MAUI in Cross-Platform Development

What is .NET Core?

.NET Core (now simply **.NET 5+**) is a **cross-platform, open-source** framework that allows C# developers to build applications for multiple operating systems.

Key   Features   of   .NET   Core:
Cross-Platform – Runs on Windows, macOS, and Linux.
High Performance – Optimized for speed and scalability.
Modular Architecture – Supports microservices and cloud-based   applications.
Open Source – Backed by a strong community.

What is .NET MAUI?

.NET Multi-platform App UI (.NET MAUI) is the successor to **Xamarin.Forms**, designed to build cross-platform **native mobile and desktop applications** using **C# and .NET**.

Key   Features   of   .NET   MAUI:
Single Codebase – Write once, deploy on Android, iOS, Windows,   and   macOS.
Native Performance – Uses platform-specific optimizations.
Unified UI Toolkit – Similar to Xamarin but with improved support for **desktop applications**.

67

How .NET MAUI Works:

- **UI Code** → Shared across platforms.
- **Native Renderers** → Adjust appearance per OS.
- **Platform-Specific Code** → Allows deeper integration (e.g., native notifications).

Example: Creating a Simple .NET MAUI App

csharp

```csharp
using Microsoft.Maui.Controls;

namespace MyMauiApp
{
    public class MainPage : ContentPage
    {
        public MainPage()
        {
            Content = new Label
            {
                Text = "Hello, .NET MAUI!",
                HorizontalOptions =
LayoutOptions.Center,
                VerticalOptions =
LayoutOptions.Center
            };
        }
    }
```

}

This single codebase runs on Windows, macOS, Android, and iOS!

2. Creating Cross-Platform Apps with Blazor, Xamarin, and Avalonia

C# offers multiple frameworks for cross-platform app development, each suited to different use cases.

Framework	Best For	Platforms Supported
.NET MAUI	Mobile & desktop apps	Windows, macOS, Android, iOS
Blazor	Web applications	Windows, macOS, Linux, Browsers
Xamarin	Mobile applications (older tech)	Android, iOS
Avalonia	Desktop UI development	Windows, macOS, Linux

1. Blazor: Web-Based Cross-Platform UI

Blazor is a **C#-based web UI framework** that allows developers to build web apps using **.NET instead of JavaScript**.

Runs on browsers (Blazor WebAssembly) or server-side (Blazor Server).
Works with WebAssembly – Enables near-native performance in browsers.
Can be used for Progressive Web Apps (PWAs).

Example: A Simple Blazor Component

```razor
@page "/hello"
<h3>Hello, Blazor!</h3>
```

Best For: Web applications, Progressive Web Apps (PWAs), internal business apps.

---

2. Xamarin (Legacy) vs. .NET MAUI

Xamarin was the original **C# cross-platform mobile framework** but has been replaced by **.NET MAUI**. **Xamarin allowed mobile app development using C# for Android and iOS. .NET MAUI is now the preferred choice**, as it extends Xamarin's capabilities to desktops.

Example: Simple Xamarin App

```csharp
using Xamarin.Forms;

namespace MyXamarinApp
{
    public class MainPage : ContentPage
    {
        public MainPage()
        {
            Content = new Label
            {
                Text = "Hello, Xamarin!",
                HorizontalOptions = LayoutOptions.Center,
                VerticalOptions = LayoutOptions.Center
            };
        }
```

```
    }
}
```

Best For: Older Xamarin projects transitioning to .NET MAUI.

---

3. Avalonia: A Modern Alternative for Desktop UI

Avalonia is an **open-source, cross-platform UI framework** that offers a modern alternative to **WPF (Windows Presentation Foundation).**

Works on Windows, macOS, and Linux. More modern UI capabilities than WPF. Follows MVVM architecture like WPF.

Example: Simple Avalonia App

```csharp
using Avalonia;
using Avalonia.Controls;
using Avalonia.Markup.Xaml;

namespace MyAvaloniaApp
{
```

```
public class MainWindow : Window
{
    public MainWindow()
    {
        Content = new TextBlock
        {
            Text = "Hello, Avalonia!",
            HorizontalAlignment                =
Avalonia.Layout.HorizontalAlignment.Center,
            VerticalAlignment                =
Avalonia.Layout.VerticalAlignment.Center
        };
    }
}
}
```

Best For: Desktop applications needing **WPF-like capabilities on Windows, macOS, and Linux**.

3. Differences Between Windows and Linux/macOS Development

1. File System & Path Differences

Windows: Uses \ as the directory separator (e.g., `C:\Users\Name\Documents`).

Linux/macOS: Uses / as the directory separator (e.g., /home/user/Documents).

Solution: Always use `Path.Combine()` instead of hardcoding paths.

csharp

```
string             path             =
Path.Combine(Environment.GetFolderPath(Environm
ent.SpecialFolder.MyDocuments), "file.txt");
```

2. Case Sensitivity

Windows: File names are case-insensitive (`MyFile.txt` and `myfile.txt` are the same).
Linux/macOS: File names are case-sensitive (`MyFile.txt` and `myfile.txt` are different).

Solution: Always handle file names carefully in cross-platform projects.

3. Executable Formats

Windows: Uses `.exe` for applications and `.dll` for shared libraries.

Linux/macOS: Uses **ELF binaries** (`chmod +x myapp` to make an executable).

Solution: Publish applications using .NET's **self-contained deployment**:

```sh

dotnet publish -r win-x64 --self-contained true
dotnet publish -r linux-x64 --self-contained true
```

---

4. Platform-Specific APIs

Some APIs are platform-specific, such as:

- **Windows Registry APIs** (Only available on Windows).
- **Mac-specific UI elements** (Not available on Windows/Linux).

Solution: Use `RuntimeInformation.IsOSPlatform()` to check the OS before calling platform-specific APIs:

```csharp

using System.Runtime.InteropServices;
```

75

```
if
(RuntimeInformation.IsOSPlatform(OSPlatform.Win
dows))
{
    Console.WriteLine("Running on Windows");
}
else                                      if
(RuntimeInformation.IsOSPlatform(OSPlatform.Lin
ux))
{
    Console.WriteLine("Running on Linux");
}
```

Summary

- **.NET Core/.NET 5+** enables **C# cross-platform development** across Windows, macOS, and Linux.
- **.NET MAUI** is the successor to Xamarin and allows **native mobile & desktop development**.
- **Blazor, Xamarin, and Avalonia** provide various options for **web, mobile, and desktop apps**.
- **Windows and Linux/macOS development differ in file handling, case sensitivity, and executable formats**.

What's Next?

In the next chapter, we'll explore **how Python and C# can work together**, integrating them in cross-platform projects to **leverage the strengths of both languages**.

CHAPTER 6

BRIDGING PYTHON AND C# TOGETHER

Python and C# are two powerful programming languages with distinct strengths. **Python excels in scripting, data science, and automation**, while **C# offers high performance, strong type safety, and seamless integration with .NET frameworks**. Combining them enables **flexibility, scalability, and efficiency** in cross-platform applications.

In this chapter, we'll explore how **Python and C# complement each other**, how to **call Python from C# using Python.NET**, how to **embed C# into Python apps**, and **real-world examples of their integration**.

---

1. How Python and C# Complement Each Other

Python and C# have **unique strengths**, making them ideal for hybrid applications.

Python Strengths

Easy to Learn & Use – Great for scripting, automation, and rapid prototyping.

Powerful Libraries – Used in **AI, data science, and machine learning** (e.g., NumPy, TensorFlow).

Cross-Platform Compatibility – Runs seamlessly on Windows, macOS, and Linux.

Great for Scripting & Automation – Can be used to automate tasks in C# applications.

C# Strengths

High Performance – Faster than Python due to static typing and Just-In-Time (JIT) compilation.

Excellent for Desktop & Web Apps – Ideal for building full-fledged applications with .NET MAUI, Blazor, and ASP.NET Core.

Strong Type Safety – Reduces runtime errors compared to Python's dynamic typing.

Seamless Windows Integration – Works well with Microsoft technologies (e.g., Azure, SQL Server, Office apps).

How They Work Well Together

Python	C#
Handles **data processing, AI, and scripting**	Manages **UI, high-performance** computing, and system integration
Used for **automation, analytics,** and **rapid** prototyping	Used for **enterprise-grade,** secure, and optimized applications
Integrates with **Jupyter Notebooks, REST APIs**	Works well with **Windows** applications, databases, and cloud services

Example **Use** **Case:** A **Python AI model** processes data and sends results to a **C# application** for a user-friendly interface.

---

2. Calling Python from C# Using Python.NET

Python.NET (also called `pythonnet`) allows **C# to interact with Python code**, enabling hybrid applications.

Installing Python.NET

Before using Python.NET, install the package via NuGet:

```sh
dotnet add package Python.Runtime
```

Ensure you have Python installed and available in your system's PATH.

Calling a Python Script from C#

The following C# code **calls a Python function** from a .py file:

```csharp
using System;
using Python.Runtime;

class Program
{
    static void Main()
    {
        // Initialize Python.NET
        PythonEngine.Initialize();

        using (Py.GIL())    // Acquire Global Interpreter Lock
        {
```

```csharp
        dynamic        pyScript        =
Py.Import("myscript");
        dynamic        result        =
pyScript.hello("C#");
        Console.WriteLine(result);
    }

        PythonEngine.Shutdown();
    }
}
```

Python script (myscript.py):

```python
python

def hello(name):
    return f"Hello from Python, {name}!"
```

This allows seamless execution of Python code inside a C# application.

Passing Data Between C# and Python

```csharp
csharp

using Python.Runtime;

using (Py.GIL())
{
```

```
dynamic numpy = Py.Import("numpy");
dynamic array = numpy.array(new int[] {1, 2,
3, 4});
Console.WriteLine(array);
}
```

This is useful for leveraging Python's NumPy and Pandas in C# applications.

---

3. Embedding C# in Python Apps

While `pythonnet` lets C# call Python, we can **also embed C# within a Python application**.

Method 1: Using Python.NET to Call C# Assemblies

This approach lets Python scripts **call C# libraries**.

Step 1: Create a C# DLL

```csharp
namespace MyCSharpLibrary
{
    public class Greeter
    {
```

```
        public   static   string   SayHello(string
name)
        {
            return $"Hello from C#, {name}!";
        }
    }
}
```

Step 2: Build and reference the DLL in Python

```python
python

import clr   # Part of pythonnet
clr.AddReference("MyCSharpLibrary")

from MyCSharpLibrary import Greeter

print(Greeter.SayHello("Python"))
```

This allows Python applications to leverage C# logic and libraries.

Method 2: Calling C# Code via REST APIs

Sometimes, it's easier to **expose C# functionality as a web service** and call it from Python.

Step 1: Create a C# Web API

```
csharp

[ApiController]
[Route("api/greet")]
public class GreetController : ControllerBase
{
    [HttpGet("{name}")]
    public string SayHello(string name)
    {
        return $"Hello from C#, {name}!";
    }
}
```

Step 2: Call the C# API from Python

```python
python

import requests

response                                        =
requests.get("http://localhost:5000/api/greet/P
ython")
print(response.text)
```

This approach is useful for cross-platform microservices.

4. Real-World Use Cases of Python and C# Integration

1. AI-Powered Desktop Applications

Scenario: A C#-based desktop application uses Python for machine learning. **C# handles UI and user interaction. Python processes AI models and returns results to C#. Example: A stock prediction app** where Python runs TensorFlow models and sends predictions to a C# dashboard.

2. Game Development

Scenario: C# (Unity) integrates with Python for **procedural content generation. Unity (C#) runs the game engine. Python scripts generate random game levels.** Example: AI-generated maps in strategy games.

3. Cloud-Based Web Services

Scenario: A **C# backend** processes client requests and **Python services** handle **data science tasks.** **C# manages the API server (ASP.NET Core).** **Python handles machine learning models.** **Example:** A **medical diagnosis web app** where a C# API calls a Python AI model for disease prediction.

4. Automating Windows Applications

Scenario: Python automates Microsoft Office tasks while C# handles **Excel-based computations.** **C# interacts with Excel via COM objects.** **Python scripts automate report generation.** **Example:** An **automated report generator** that fills Excel spreadsheets using **C# and Python.**

Summary

- **Python and C# complement each other** in hybrid applications.
- **Python.NET enables calling Python from C#,** useful for data processing and automation.

- **C# can be embedded into Python apps** using `clr.AddReference()` or via REST APIs.
- **Real-world use cases include AI-powered applications, game development, web services, and Windows automation.**

What's Next?

In the next chapter, we'll **build real-world Python-C# applications**, covering **step-by-step implementation and best practices**!

PART 3

BUILDING CROSS-PLATFORM APPLICATIONS

CHAPTER 7

DEVELOPING CLI APPLICATIONS IN PYTHON AND C#

Command-line interface (CLI) applications are powerful tools in software engineering. They provide efficient automation, scripting capabilities, and integration with other systems. Both **Python** and **C# (.NET Core)** offer robust options for building cross-platform CLI applications.

In this chapter, we'll explore:
Why CLI apps are important in modern software engineering.
How to build CLI apps using Python's argparse and Click.
How to develop CLI tools in C# using .NET Core.

---

1. Why CLI Apps Matter in Software Engineering

CLI applications are widely used for:

- **Automation & Scripting:** Repetitive tasks like file management, deployments, and data processing.
- **DevOps & System Administration:** Running shell scripts, server monitoring, and managing cloud infrastructure.
- **Developer Tools:** Version control (e.g., Git), package managers (e.g., npm, pip, NuGet), and debugging tools.
- **Data Processing:** Running ETL (Extract, Transform, Load) pipelines or AI model training jobs.

Examples of Popular CLI Applications:

CLI App	Purpose	Technology Used
Git	Version Control	C
Docker	Container Management	Go
pip	Python Package Manager	Python
dotnet CLI	.NET Project Management	C#
AWS CLI	Cloud Management	Python

CLI apps are **lightweight, fast, and easy to use**, making them essential in cross-platform development.

2. Building CLI Applications in Python

Python is one of the best languages for CLI development due to its simplicity and extensive libraries. The two main options for creating command-line applications in Python are **argparse** (built-in) and **Click** (third-party).

Using argparse (Standard Library)

argparse is a **built-in module** for handling command-line arguments in Python.

Example: Basic CLI App Using argparse

```python
python

import argparse

# Create argument parser
parser = argparse.ArgumentParser(description="A
simple CLI calculator")

# Define arguments
parser.add_argument("num1",          type=float,
help="First number")
parser.add_argument("num2",          type=float,
help="Second number")
```

```python
parser.add_argument("--operation",
choices=["add", "subtract", "multiply",
"divide"], default="add", help="Operation to
perform")

# Parse arguments
args = parser.parse_args()

# Perform calculations
if args.operation == "add":
    result = args.num1 + args.num2
elif args.operation == "subtract":
    result = args.num1 - args.num2
elif args.operation == "multiply":
    result = args.num1 * args.num2
elif args.operation == "divide":
    result = args.num1 / args.num2

print(f"Result: {result}")
```

Usage in Terminal:

```sh
sh
```

```sh
python calculator.py 10 5 --operation multiply
```

Output:

```makefile
makefile
```

```
Result: 50.0
```

Using Click (More User-Friendly)

Click is a powerful third-party library that simplifies CLI creation.

Installation:

```sh
pip install click
```

Example: CLI App Using Click

```python
import click

@click.command()
@click.argument("num1", type=float)
@click.argument("num2", type=float)
@click.option("--operation",
type=click.Choice(["add",         "subtract",
"multiply",      "divide"]),      default="add",
help="Operation to perform")
def calculate(num1, num2, operation):
    """Simple CLI calculator using Click"""
    if operation == "add":
```

94

```
        result = num1 + num2
    elif operation == "subtract":
        result = num1 - num2
    elif operation == "multiply":
        result = num1 * num2
    elif operation == "divide":
        result = num1 / num2

    click.echo(f"Result: {result}")

if __name__ == "__main__":
    calculate()
```

Usage in Terminal:

```sh
```

```
python calculator.py 10 5 --operation subtract
```

Click provides better user feedback, validation, and error handling.

---

3. Building CLI Applications in C# Using .NET Core

.NET Core (now .NET 6+) provides a rich set of tools for building cross-platform CLI applications.

Basic CLI App in C#

Create a new .NET CLI project:

```sh
```

```
dotnet new console -n MyCliApp
cd MyCliApp
```

Modify Program.cs to accept command-line arguments:

```csharp
```

```
using System;

class Program
{
    static void Main(string[] args)
    {
        if (args.Length < 3)
        {
            Console.WriteLine("Usage: dotnet run <num1> <num2> --operation add/subtract/multiply/divide");
            return;
        }

        double num1 = Convert.ToDouble(args[0]);
        double num2 = Convert.ToDouble(args[1]);
```

96

```
        string operation = args[2];

        double result = operation switch
        {
            "add" => num1 + num2,
            "subtract" => num1 - num2,
            "multiply" => num1 * num2,
            "divide" => num1 / num2,
            _           =>          throw          new
ArgumentException("Invalid operation")
        };

        Console.WriteLine($"Result: {result}");
    }
}
```

Run the CLI App in Terminal:

```sh

dotnet run 10 5 subtract
```

Output:

```makefile

Result: 5
```

Using Spectre.Console for Advanced CLI Apps

Spectre.Console is a **third-party library** that allows for **rich CLI UIs** with colors, tables, and progress bars.

Installation:

```sh

dotnet add package Spectre.Console
```

Example: CLI App with Spectre.Console

```csharp

using System;
using Spectre.Console;

class Program
{
    static void Main()
    {
        var operation = AnsiConsole.Prompt(
            new SelectionPrompt<string>()
                .Title("Choose an operation:")
                .AddChoices("Add",    "Subtract",
"Multiply", "Divide"));

        double         num1         =
AnsiConsole.Ask<double>("Enter first number:");
```

```
        double            num2           =
AnsiConsole.Ask<double>("Enter second number:");

        double result = operation switch
        {
            "Add" => num1 + num2,
            "Subtract" => num1 - num2,
            "Multiply" => num1 * num2,
            "Divide" => num1 / num2,
            _            =>           throw          new
ArgumentException("Invalid operation")
        };

        AnsiConsole.MarkupLine($"[green]Result:
{result}[/]");
    }
}
```

Spectre.Console allows for a more interactive CLI experience.

4. Python vs. C# for CLI Development

Feature	Python	C# (.NET Core)
Ease of Use	Simple, beginner-friendly	More structured, requires compilation
Performance	Slower	Faster due to JIT compilation
Libraries	`argparse`, `Click`, `Typer`	`System.CommandLine`, `Spectre.Console`
Cross-Platform	Yes	Yes, with .NET Core

When to Choose Python: Best for **quick prototyping, automation, and DevOps scripts**.

Recommended for **data science, machine learning, and web scraping CLI tools**.

When to Choose C#: Ideal for **enterprise applications, system utilities, and high-performance tools**.

Best when **integrating with .NET ecosystem or requiring Windows-specific functionalities**.

Summary

- **CLI apps are essential** for automation, DevOps, and development tools.
- **Python** offers simplicity with **argparse and Click**.
- **C#** provides performance and **rich CLI experiences** with .NET Core and Spectre.Console.
- **Python is best for scripting and automation**, while C# **is ideal for enterprise-grade CLI tools**.

What's Next?

In the next chapter, we'll explore **how to create cross-platform GUI applications** using **Python's PyQt/Kivy and C#'s .NET MAUI/Avalonia!**

CHAPTER 8

CREATING GUI APPLICATIONS FOR MULTIPLE PLATFORMS

Graphical User Interface (GUI) applications provide a more intuitive way for users to interact with software. In cross-platform development, selecting the right **GUI framework** is critical for ensuring **compatibility, performance, and user experience** across Windows, macOS, and Linux.

In this chapter, we'll explore: **Python GUI frameworks:** Tkinter, PyQt, Kivy **C# GUI frameworks:** WPF, Avalonia, .NET MAUI **Best practices for designing cross-platform UIs**

1. Python GUI Frameworks

Python offers multiple options for **developing cross-platform GUI applications**. The three most commonly used frameworks are **Tkinter, PyQt, and Kivy**.

1.1 Tkinter (Built-in GUI Framework)

102

Best for: Simple desktop applications, lightweight tools

Platforms: Windows, macOS, Linux

Comes built-in with Python (no extra installation needed)

Ideal for small utilities and educational purposes

Limited in terms of modern UI elements

Example: Basic Tkinter Application

```python

import tkinter as tk

root = tk.Tk()
root.title("Cross-Platform Tkinter App")
root.geometry("300x200")

label = tk.Label(root, text="Hello, Tkinter!")
label.pack()

root.mainloop()
```

Pros: Easy to learn, no dependencies

Cons: Outdated look, lacks modern UI components

1.2 PyQt (Feature-Rich GUI Framework)

Best for: Full-featured desktop applications with a professional UI

Platforms: Windows, macOS, Linux

Provides modern UI components

Excellent for large-scale applications

Requires commercial licensing for proprietary software

Installation:

sh

```
pip install PyQt5
```

Example: Basic PyQt Application

python

```
from PyQt5.QtWidgets import QApplication,
QLabel, QWidget
import sys

app = QApplication(sys.argv)
window = QWidget()
window.setWindowTitle("PyQt Cross-Platform App")
window.setGeometry(100, 100, 300, 200)

label = QLabel("Hello, PyQt!", window)
label.move(100, 90)
```

```
window.show()
sys.exit(app.exec_())
```

Pros: Modern UI, highly customizable

Cons: Can be complex for beginners

1.3 Kivy (Best for Mobile & Touch-Based Apps)

Best for: Mobile and touch-enabled applications
Platforms: Windows, macOS, Linux, Android, iOS
Great for mobile app development
Multi-touch support and GPU acceleration
UI looks non-native, requires additional styling

Installation:

```sh
pip install kivy
```

Example: Basic Kivy Application

```python
from kivy.app import App
```

```
from kivy.uix.label import Label

class MyApp(App):
    def build(self):
        return Label(text="Hello, Kivy!")

MyApp().run()
```

Pros: Cross-platform including mobile
Cons: Custom UI (not native-looking), higher learning curve

---

2. C# GUI Frameworks

C# offers multiple options for **developing cross-platform desktop applications**, with **WPF, Avalonia, and .NET MAUI** being the most widely used.

2.1 WPF (Windows Presentation Foundation)

Best for: Native Windows applications
Platforms: **Windows-only**
Modern UI with XAML-based design
Supports **data binding and MVVM architecture**
Not cross-platform (Windows only)

Example: Basic WPF App (`MainWindow.xaml`)

```xml
xml

<Window x:Class="WpfApp.MainWindow"

xmlns="http://schemas.microsoft.com/winfx/2006/
xaml/presentation"

xmlns:x="http://schemas.microsoft.com/winfx/200
6/xaml"
        Title="WPF        App"        Height="200"
Width="300">
    <Grid>
        <TextBlock Text="Hello, WPF!"
                HorizontalAlignment="Center"
                VerticalAlignment="Center"
                FontSize="16"/>
    </Grid>
</Window>
```

Pros: Rich UI, MVVM support
Cons: Windows-only

2.2 Avalonia (Cross-Platform WPF Alternative)

Best for: Desktop applications that require WPF-like features

Platforms: Windows, macOS, Linux
Similar to WPF but cross-platform
Uses XAML for UI design
Slightly smaller community support than WPF

Installation:

sh

```
dotnet new avalonia.app -n MyAvaloniaApp
```

Example: Basic Avalonia App (`MainWindow.axaml`)

xml

```xml
<Window xmlns="https://github.com/avaloniaui"
        Title="Avalonia App" Width="300"
Height="200">
    <TextBlock Text="Hello, Avalonia!"
            HorizontalAlignment="Center"
            VerticalAlignment="Center"/>
</Window>
```

Pros: WPF-like development but cross-platform
Cons: Not as mature as WPF

2.3 .NET MAUI (Successor to Xamarin)

Best for: Cross-platform mobile and desktop applications

Platforms: Windows, macOS, Android, iOS

Supports native UI elements for each platform

Fully integrated with .NET

Still evolving; requires .NET 6+

Example: Basic .NET MAUI App

```csharp
using Microsoft.Maui.Controls;

namespace MyMauiApp
{
    public class MainPage : ContentPage
    {
        public MainPage()
        {
            Content = new Label
            {
                Text = "Hello, .NET MAUI!",
                HorizontalOptions = LayoutOptions.Center,
```

```
                    VerticalOptions                    =
LayoutOptions.Center
            };
        }
    }
}
```

Pros: Mobile and desktop support in one framework

Cons: Requires learning new concepts

---

3. Best Practices for Designing Cross-Platform UIs

When designing cross-platform GUI applications, follow these best practices:

1. Use Adaptive Layouts

Ensure that the UI adapts well to different screen sizes and operating systems. **Python:** Use `pack()` and `grid()` in Tkinter, or `QVBoxLayout` in PyQt. **C#:** Use **Responsive Layouts** in .NET MAUI or Avalonia.

2. Follow Platform-Specific UI Guidelines

Respect platform-specific **design conventions**:

- **Windows** – Uses Fluent Design System
- **macOS** – Uses macOS Human Interface Guidelines
- **Linux** – Supports various DEs (GNOME, KDE)

3. Prioritize Performance

- **Optimize rendering** by using hardware acceleration (e.g., Kivy, Avalonia).
- **Minimize memory usage** by reusing UI components.

4. Implement MVVM (Model-View-ViewModel) Pattern

For better **code organization and UI logic separation**, use **MVVM**:

- **C#:** Common in **WPF, Avalonia, .NET MAUI**
- **Python:** Implement using **PyQt's Model-View framework**.

5. Ensure Accessibility

Add support for **keyboard navigation and screen readers**. Use **color contrast and font scaling** for better UX.

Summary

- **Python GUI frameworks:**
  - **Tkinter** (lightweight, built-in)
  - **PyQt** (modern, powerful)
  - **Kivy** (best for mobile & touchscreens)
- **C# GUI frameworks:**
  - **WPF** (Windows only, rich UI)
  - **Avalonia** (cross-platform alternative to WPF)
  - **.NET MAUI** (for mobile & desktop apps)
- **Best practices include using adaptive layouts, optimizing performance, and following platform-specific UI guidelines.**

What's Next?

In the next chapter, we'll dive into **cross-platform web development using Python (Django, Flask) and C# (ASP.NET Core, Blazor).**

CHAPTER 9

WEB DEVELOPMENT WITH PYTHON AND C#

Web development is one of the most common use cases for both **Python** and **C#**. Python is widely used for **rapid backend development** with frameworks like **Django and Flask**, while C# provides **high-performance web applications** using **ASP.NET Core**.

In this chapter, we'll explore: **Python's Django & Flask for back-end development C# ASP.NET Core for high-performance web applications Hosting web applications on cloud platforms**

---

1. Python's Django & Flask for Backend Development

Python is an excellent language for building web applications due to its simplicity and rich ecosystem. Two of the most popular **Python web frameworks** are **Django** and **Flask**.

1.1 Django: The "Batteries-Included" Web Framework

Best for: Large, scalable web applications (e.g., e-commerce, enterprise apps). Comes with built-in ORM, authentication, admin panel. Secure and scalable. Great for **database-driven applications**. Can be overkill for small projects.

Installation:

sh

```
pip install django
```

Example: Creating a Simple Django Web App

sh

```
django-admin startproject myproject
cd myproject
python manage.py runserver
```

Visit `http://127.0.0.1:8000/` to see your Django site running.

Example: Simple Django View (`views.py`)

```python
python

from django.http import HttpResponse

def home(request):
    return HttpResponse("Hello, Django!")
```

Django is ideal for full-stack applications with built-in database support.

1.2 Flask: The Lightweight Web Framework

Best for: Small and fast applications, REST APIs. Minimalistic, only includes what you need. Great for **REST API development**. Requires third-party libraries for advanced features.

Installation:

```sh
sh

pip install flask
```

Example: Simple Flask App

```python
python
```

115

```
from flask import Flask

app = Flask(__name__)

@app.route("/")
def home():
    return "Hello, Flask!"

if __name__ == "__main__":
    app.run(debug=True)
```

Run the app:

```sh
sh
```

```
python app.py
```

Flask is great for building REST APIs and microservices.

---

2. C# ASP.NET Core for High-Performance Web Apps

ASP.NET Core is a **cross-platform, high-performance web framework** for building **modern web applications and APIs**.

2.1 Why Use ASP.NET Core?

116

Cross-Platform – Runs on Windows, macOS, and Linux.

High Performance – Outperforms many other web frameworks.

Built-in Dependency Injection – Helps manage app components   efficiently.

Great for Enterprise Applications – Used in financial systems, e-commerce, and SaaS products.

2.2 Creating a Simple ASP.NET Core Web App

Step 1: Create a new ASP.NET Core project

```sh
```

```
dotnet new web -n MyWebApp
cd MyWebApp
dotnet run
```

Visit `http://localhost:5000/` to see your ASP.NET Core app running.

Step 2: Modify `Program.cs` to Add a Basic Web Page

```csharp
```

```
var                    builder              =
WebApplication.CreateBuilder(args);
var app = builder.Build();

app.MapGet("/", () => "Hello, ASP.NET Core!");

app.Run();
```

This simple web app responds with "Hello, ASP.NET Core!" when accessed.

2.3 Building a REST API with ASP.NET Core

Step 1: Create an API Project

```sh
sh

dotnet new webapi -n MyApi
cd MyApi
dotnet run
```

Step 2: Modify Controllers/WeatherForecastController.cs

```csharp
csharp

using Microsoft.AspNetCore.Mvc;
```

118

```
[ApiController]
[Route("api/hello")]
public class HelloController : ControllerBase
{
    [HttpGet]
    public string Get()
    {
        return "Hello from ASP.NET Core API!";
    }
}
```

Run the API and visit `http://localhost:5000/api/hello` **in your browser.**

---

3. Hosting Web Applications on Cloud Platforms

Once your **Python Django/Flask app** or **ASP.NET Core web app** is ready, you'll need to deploy it online.

3.1 Hosting Python Web Applications

Cloud Provider	Best For	Deployment Method
Heroku	Quick & simple deployments	`git push heroku main`
AWS (EC2, Lambda)	Scalable production apps	EC2 instances, AWS Lambda
Google Cloud (App Engine)	Serverless applications	`gcloud app deploy`
Azure App Service	Enterprise Django/Flask apps	Azure CLI

Deploying a Flask App to Heroku

1. Install the Heroku CLI:

```sh
pip install gunicorn
```

2. Create a `Procfile`:

```makefile
web: gunicorn app:app
```

120

3. Deploy the app:

```sh
git init
heroku create myflaskapp
git add .
git commit -m "Initial commit"
git push heroku main
```

Your Flask app is now live on Heroku!

3.2 Hosting ASP.NET Core Applications

Cloud Provider	Best For	Deployment Method
Azure App Service	Enterprise applications	`az webapp deploy`
AWS (Elastic Beanstalk, EC2)	Scalable web apps	`dotnet publish` & upload
Google Cloud Run	Serverless .NET apps	`gcloud deploy`

Deploying an ASP.NET Core App to Azure

1. Login to Azure CLI:

```sh
```

```sh
az login
```

2. Create an Azure Web App:

```sh
```

```sh
az webapp create --resource-group
MyResourceGroup --plan MyPlan --name
MyAspNetApp --runtime DOTNETCORE:6.0
```

3. Deploy the app:

```sh
```

```sh
az webapp deploy --name MyAspNetApp --src-
path ./publish
```

Your ASP.NET Core app is now live on Azure!

4. Python vs. C# for Web Development

Feature	Python (Django/Flask)	C# (ASP.NET Core)
Ease of Use	Simple & beginner-friendly	More structured & robust
Performance	Slower for large applications	High performance
Best For	Rapid development, data-driven apps	Enterprise apps, APIs
Deployment	Heroku, AWS, Google Cloud	Azure, AWS, Google Cloud

Choose Python if you need **rapid development, simpler syntax, and lightweight APIs.** **Choose C#** if you need **high-performance, enterprise-level applications**.

Summary

- **Python (Django & Flask)** provides easy and fast web development.

- **C# ASP.NET Core** offers high performance and enterprise-ready features.
- **Hosting options include Heroku, AWS, Azure, and Google Cloud.**
- **Python is great for data-driven and lightweight web apps**, while **C# is ideal for large-scale, high-performance applications.**

What's Next?

In the next chapter, we'll explore **mobile app development** using **Python (Kivy, BeeWare) and C# (.NET MAUI, Xamarin)**!

CHAPTER 10

MOBILE APP DEVELOPMENT WITH PYTHON AND C#

Mobile applications are an essential part of modern software development, enabling businesses and individuals to interact with technology on-the-go. **Python and C#** both provide cross-platform mobile development frameworks, allowing developers to write **one codebase** and deploy it to **iOS and Android**.

In this chapter, we'll explore: **Python frameworks:** Kivy, BeeWare
C# solutions: Xamarin, .NET MAUI
When to use Python vs. C# for mobile apps

---

1. Python Frameworks for Mobile Development

Python is not the most common language for mobile development, but frameworks like **Kivy and BeeWare** make it possible.

125

1.1 Kivy: The Most Popular Python Mobile Framework

Best for: Touch-based applications, multimedia apps, prototypes

Platforms: Android, iOS, Windows, macOS, Linux

Cross-platform UI components

Supports OpenGL for GPU-accelerated graphics

Touchscreen and multi-touch support

UI elements are not native

Larger app size due to Python interpreter bundling

Installation:

sh

```
pip install kivy
```

Example: Simple Kivy App

python

```
from kivy.app import App
from kivy.uix.label import Label

class MyApp(App):
    def build(self):
```

126

```
return Label(text="Hello, Kivy!")
```

```
MyApp().run()
```

How to package for Android?
Use **Buildozer** to compile your Python Kivy app into an APK:

sh

```
pip install buildozer
buildozer init
buildozer -v android debug
```

Output: `myapp.apk` ready for installation on Android.

1.2 BeeWare: Native-Looking Python Apps

Best for: Native UI applications for Android, iOS, and desktop

Platforms: iOS, Android, Windows, macOS, Linux
Uses **native UI elements** for a **true native look**
Supports **iOS (unlike Kivy, which is harder to run on iOS)**
Lightweight compared to Kivy

Not as mature or feature-rich as Kivy
iOS development requires **Xcode and macOS**

Installation:

sh

```
pip install briefcase
```

Example: Simple BeeWare App

python

```
from toga import App, MainWindow

def main(app):
    return MainWindow(title="Hello, BeeWare!")

app = App("BeeWare App", "com.example.bee")
app.main_loop(main)
```

How to package for Android?

sh

```
briefcase create android
briefcase build android
briefcase run android
```

Output: A **native Android app** with a small footprint.

---

2. C# Solutions for Mobile Development

C# is a **stronger** language for mobile development, with **Xamarin and .NET MAUI** providing full-featured frameworks for **native and cross-platform mobile apps**.

2.1 Xamarin: The Older but Still Used Framework

Best for: Legacy cross-platform mobile applications **Platforms:** **Android,** **iOS,** **Windows** Uses **C# and .NET**, reducing code duplication Allows **platform-specific** **optimizations** **Access to native APIs** like camera, GPS, etc. Microsoft is shifting towards **.NET MAUI**, meaning Xamarin's future is limited

Example: Xamarin.Forms App

```csharp

using Xamarin.Forms;

namespace MyXamarinApp
```

```
{

    public class App : Application
    {

        public App()
        {

            MainPage = new ContentPage
            {

                Content = new Label
                {

                    Text = "Hello, Xamarin!",
                    HorizontalOptions       =
LayoutOptions.Center,
                    VerticalOptions         =
LayoutOptions.Center
                }
            };
        }
    }
}
```

Deploy on Android or iOS with Visual Studio

1. Open the Xamarin project in **Visual Studio**.
2. Select **Android Emulator or iOS Simulator**.
3. Click **Run** to launch the app.

2.2 .NET MAUI: The Future of Cross-Platform Mobile Development

Best for: Modern cross-platform applications
**Platforms: Android, iOS, Windows, macOS
Successor to Xamarin**, integrates with .NET 6+
Unified UI framework (similar to Xamarin.Forms)
Supports native APIs while keeping a single codebase
Requires **.NET 6 or later**, not compatible with older .NET versions

Installation:

```sh

dotnet new maui -n MyMauiApp
cd MyMauiApp
dotnet build
```

Example: Simple .NET MAUI App

```csharp

using Microsoft.Maui.Controls;

namespace MyMauiApp
{
    public class MainPage : ContentPage
```

131

```
    {
        public MainPage()
        {
            Content = new Label
            {
                Text = "Hello, .NET MAUI!",
                HorizontalOptions          =
LayoutOptions.Center,
                VerticalOptions            =
LayoutOptions.Center
            };
        }
    }
}
```

How to deploy?

1. Open the .NET MAUI project in **Visual Studio 2022.**
2. Select **Android, iOS, or Windows** as the target.
3. Click **Run** to launch the app.

3. When to Use Python vs. C# for Mobile Apps

Both **Python and C#** can be used for mobile applications, but they have different use cases.

132

Feature	Python (Kivy, BeeWare)	C# (.NET MAUI, Xamarin)
Ease of Use	Easier for beginners	Requires learning .NET MAUI/XAML
Performance	Slower due to Python interpreter	Faster, compiled into native code
UI Look & Feel	Kivy: Custom UI, BeeWare: Native UI	Fully native UI with native components
Best For	Prototypes, automation, lightweight apps	Full-fledged, enterprise-grade mobile apps
iOS Support	BeeWare (Yes), Kivy (Harder)	Fully supported via .NET MAUI
Android Support	Yes	Yes
Deployment Complexity	Requires Buildozer (Android), Xcode (iOS)	Easier deployment with Visual Studio

Choose Python if: You need **quick prototypes** or **lightweight** **apps**.

You are working on **automation tools** that require a mobile interface.

You are familiar with Python but **not C#**.

Choose C# if: You need **high-performance, enterprise-grade** mobile apps.
You want **native UI and access to device APIs**.
You are targeting **Windows + mobile** with **one codebase**.

---

4. Summary

- **Python Mobile Development:**
  - **Kivy**: Best for quick prototyping and **custom UI apps**.
  - **BeeWare**: Best for **native UI apps** on iOS, Android, and desktop.
- **C# Mobile Development:**
  - **Xamarin**: Still in use, but being replaced by **.NET MAUI**.
  - **.NET MAUI**: The **future of cross-platform mobile development** with full **native support**.
- **When to Choose Python vs. C#:**
  - **Use Python for smaller, quick projects and automation.**

o **Use C# for scalable, high-performance enterprise apps.**

.NET MAUI is currently the best framework for cross-platform mobile development due to its **native performance and Microsoft support**.

What's Next?

In the next chapter, we'll explore **game development using Python (Pygame, Godot) and C# (Unity, MonoGame)**!

CHAPTER 11

GAME DEVELOPMENT ACROSS PLATFORMS

Game development is one of the most exciting areas in software engineering, allowing developers to create engaging experiences for **PCs, consoles, and mobile devices**. **Python and C#** both offer **cross-platform game development** capabilities, with frameworks like **Godot (Python/C#), Unity (C#), and Pygame (Python)** making game creation accessible to developers of all skill levels.

In this chapter, we'll explore: **Unity (C#) vs. Godot (Python/C#) for game development Writing cross-platform game logic Performance considerations in game development**

---

1. Using Unity (C#) vs. Godot (Python/C#)

Unity and Godot are two of the most widely used cross-platform game engines, but they have distinct differences.

1.1 Unity (C#)

Best for: Professional and commercial game development

Platforms: Windows, macOS, Linux, Android, iOS, Web, **Consoles**

Industry standard, used by indie and AAA developers

C# **scripting** for game logic

Asset Store provides thousands of game assets and plugins

High-performance rendering with Unity's DOTS (Data-Oriented **Tech** **Stack)**

Can be **heavy** **on** **system** **resources**

Licensing changes (recent Unity fees) may impact indie developers

Example: Simple Unity Game (C# Script)

```csharp
using UnityEngine;

public class PlayerMovement : MonoBehaviour
{
    public float speed = 5f;

    void Update()
    {
```

```
     float move = Input.GetAxis("Horizontal")
* speed * Time.deltaTime;
     transform.Translate(move, 0, 0);
  }
}
```

Attach this script to a GameObject in Unity, and it will move left and right with keyboard input.

1.2 Godot (Python/GDScript/C#)

Best for: Lightweight game development, open-source projects

Platforms: Windows, macOS, Linux, Android, iOS, Web

Uses **GDScript (Python-like)** or **C#** for scripting

Smaller,   faster,   and   open-source

Built-in   2D   and   3D   physics   engine

Smaller   community compared   to   Unity

Fewer **third-party assets**

Example: Simple Godot Script (GDScript)

```
gdscript

extends KinematicBody2D
```

138

```
var speed = 200

func _physics_process(delta):
    var velocity = Vector2()
    if Input.is_action_pressed("ui_right"):
        velocity.x += speed
    if Input.is_action_pressed("ui_left"):
        velocity.x -= speed
    move_and_slide(velocity)
```

This script moves an object left and right in a Godot 2D game.

Unity vs. Godot: Comparison

Feature	Unity (C#)	Godot (GDScript/Python/C#)
Best For	3D & professional game development	2D indie & open-source games
Scripting	C#	GDScript (Python-like) & C#
Performance	High, but resource-heavy	Lightweight & optimized

Feature	Unity (C#)	Godot (GDScript/Python/C#)
Platforms	Windows, macOS, Linux, Mobile, Web, Consoles	Windows, macOS, Linux, Mobile, Web
Asset Store	Extensive third-party assets	Limited assets
Ease of Learning	Steeper learning curve	Easier for beginners
Licensing	Commercial fees for Unity Pro	Completely free & open-source

Choose Unity if: You need a **AAA-quality game engine**, access to a large community, and professional tools. **Choose Godot if:** You prefer an **open-source, lightweight, beginner-friendly engine** for 2D/3D games.

2. Writing Cross-Platform Game Logic

Game logic should be **independent of platform-specific code** to allow smooth cross-platform deployment.

140

2.1 Input Handling

Handle player input generically to work across different devices. **Unity (C#) Example:**

```csharp
csharp

if (Input.GetKey(KeyCode.Space))
{
    Debug.Log("Jump!");
}
```

Godot (GDScript) Example:

```gdscript
gdscript

if Input.is_action_pressed("jump"):
    print("Jump!")
```

Use input mapping so the game logic stays consistent across platforms.

2.2 Using Physics Engines

Most game engines have built-in physics engines that work across platforms.

141

Unity 2D Physics (C#)

```csharp
Rigidbody2D rb;

void Start()
{
    rb = GetComponent<Rigidbody2D>();
}

void Update()
{
    if (Input.GetKeyDown(KeyCode.Space))
    {
        rb.AddForce(Vector2.up          *          5,
ForceMode2D.Impulse);
    }
}
```

Works identically across Windows, macOS, Linux, Android, and iOS.

Godot 2D Physics (GDScript)

```gdscript
extends RigidBody2D
```

```
func _ready():
    pass


func _input(event):
    if event.is_action_pressed("jump"):
        apply_impulse(Vector2.ZERO, Vector2(0, -
200))
```

2.3 Networking for Multiplayer Games

If your game supports **multiplayer**, you need a **cross-platform networking solution**.

Unity Netcode for GameObjects

```csharp
using Unity.Netcode;

public class PlayerController : NetworkBehaviour
{
    public override void OnNetworkSpawn()
    {
        if (IsOwner)
        {
            Debug.Log("This is my player!");
        }
    }
```

```
}
```

Supports **Windows, macOS, Linux, consoles, and mobile**.

Godot Multiplayer

```gdscript
gdscript

extends Node

func _ready():
    var peer = NetworkedMultiplayerENet.new()
    peer.create_server(12345, 10)
    get_tree().set_network_peer(peer)
```

Supports **LAN and online multiplayer** across platforms.

---

3. Performance Considerations in Game Development

Game performance is **critical** for a smooth player experience, especially in **cross-platform games**.

3.1 Optimizing Rendering

- **Use efficient textures and models** to reduce memory usage.
- **Limit draw calls** (batch rendering whenever possible).

- **Use Object Pooling** to reduce memory allocation.

Unity Optimization (C#)

csharp

```
QualitySettings.SetQualityLevel(2);
Application.targetFrameRate = 60;
```

Godot Optimization (GDScript)

gdscript

```
get_tree().set_screen_stretch(SceneTree.STRETCH
_MODE_2D,          SceneTree.STRETCH_ASPECT_KEEP,
Vector2(1920, 1080))
```

3.2 Reducing CPU Usage

- **Avoid frequent memory allocation** (use object pooling).
- **Use coroutines and async processing** to prevent blocking.

Unity Coroutine Example

csharp

```
IEnumerator WaitAndShoot()
```

145

```
{
    yield return new WaitForSeconds(1f);
    Shoot();
}
```

Godot Coroutine Example

```
gdscript
```

```
yield(get_tree().create_timer(1.0), "timeout")
shoot()
```

Asynchronous execution improves performance on all platforms.

3.3 Choosing the Right Platform

Platform	Best For	Game Engine
Windows	PC games, Steam releases	Unity, Godot
macOS	Casual & indie games	Godot, Unity
Linux	Open-source & niche games	Godot
Android/iOS	Mobile gaming	Unity, Godot

146

Platform	Best For	Game Engine
Web	Browser-based games	Godot, Unity WebGL

Unity is best for complex, high-performance games. Godot is better for 2D, mobile, and indie projects.

4. Summary

- **Unity (C#) is the industry standard for professional game development.**
- **Godot (Python/C#) is a great open-source alternative for indie and 2D games.**
- **Game logic should be platform-independent** to ensure smooth cross-platform deployment.
- **Performance optimizations** (rendering, physics, networking) improve game quality.

What's Next?

In the next chapter, we'll explore **desktop application development**, including **packaging apps for Windows, macOS, and Linux**!

PART 4
CROSS-PLATFORM SYSTEMS & FRAMEWORKS

CHAPTER 12

CROSS-PLATFORM DESKTOP APPLICATION DEVELOPMENT

Developing desktop applications that run on **Windows, macOS, and Linux** requires **cross-platform frameworks** that ensure compatibility without rewriting code for each operating system. Choosing the right tool depends on **performance, UI needs, and platform requirements**.

In this chapter, we'll explore:
Packaging desktop apps for Windows, macOS, and Linux
Comparing Electron, .NET MAUI, and PyQt for cross-platform desktop development
Performance considerations in desktop applications

1. Packaging Desktop Apps for Windows, macOS, and Linux

Once an application is built, it must be **packaged** so users can install and run it without requiring additional dependencies.

1.1 Packaging Python Desktop Applications

For **Python GUI applications** (built with PyQt, Tkinter, or Kivy), we use **PyInstaller** or **cx_Freeze**.

Install PyInstaller:

```sh
pip install pyinstaller
```

Create a standalone executable:

```sh
pyinstaller --onefile --windowed myapp.py
```

Generates an .exe for Windows, .app for macOS, or ELF binary for Linux.

Example Packaging for macOS:

```sh
```

```
pyinstaller --onefile --windowed --name "MyApp"
myapp.py
```

Output: `dist/MyApp.app`

Example Packaging for Linux:

```sh
```

```
pyinstaller --onefile myapp.py
```

Output: `dist/myapp`

! Issues & Fixes:

- **Linux users may need additional dependencies** (`apt install build-essential`)
- **macOS apps need signing** (`codesign -s "Developer ID" MyApp.app`)

 Use **PyInstaller** for **Python apps requiring cross-platform distribution.**

1.2 Packaging .NET MAUI Desktop Applications

.NET MAUI allows **C# developers** to build native desktop applications for **Windows, macOS, and Linux**.

Publish for Windows:

```sh
dotnet publish -c Release -r win-x64 --self-contained true
```

Publish for macOS:

```sh
dotnet publish -c Release -r osx-x64 --self-contained true
```

Publish for Linux:

```sh
dotnet publish -c Release -r linux-x64 --self-contained true
```

.NET MAUI produces native installers (`.msi`, `.dmg`, `.deb`) for each OS.

1.3 Packaging Electron Applications

Electron allows developers to build **desktop applications using web technologies** (HTML, CSS, JavaScript).

Install Electron Packager:

sh

```
npm install -g electron-packager
```

Create an Electron App:

sh

```
electron-packager . MyElectronApp --platform=win32 --arch=x64
```

Creates an **Electron .exe for Windows**.

Package for macOS:

sh

```
electron-packager . MyElectronApp --platform=darwin --arch=x64
```

Produces a **macOS .app bundle**.

Package for Linux:

```sh
electron-packager . MyElectronApp --platform=linux --arch=x64
```

Produces a **Linux** `.deb` **or** `.AppImage`.

! Issues & Fixes:

- **Large app size** (Electron bundles Chromium, making `.exe` files large).
- **Higher memory usage than native apps**.

Use Electron if you need a web-based desktop UI.

---

2. Electron vs. .NET MAUI vs. PyQt: Choosing the Right Tool

Each **cross-platform desktop development framework** has strengths and weaknesses.

Feature	Electron (JS)	.NET MAUI (C#)	PyQt (Python)
Best For	Web-based desktop apps	Native UI apps	Python-powered desktop apps
Performance	**Slow** (runs on Chromium)	**Fast** (native performance)	**Fast** (compiled to native)
App Size	**Large** (~50MB+)	**Medium** (~20MB)	**Small** (~10MB)
UI Framework	HTML, CSS, JS	XAML, C#	Qt Widgets
Access to OS Features	Requires extra APIs	Full access	Full access
Cross-Platform Support	Yes	Yes	Yes
Ease of Development	Easy for web developers	Requires .NET knowledge	Requires Python + Qt knowledge

155

Feature	Electron (JS)	.NET MAUI (C#)	PyQt (Python)
Memory Usage	High (~200MB+)	Low (~50MB)	Low (~50MB)

Choose Electron if:

- You're comfortable with **HTML, CSS, and JavaScript.**
- You want to build a **web-based desktop app.**
- You don't mind **high memory usage.**

Choose .NET MAUI if:

- You need a **native-looking, high-performance** app.
- You are building for **Windows/macOS/Linux with native UI elements.**
- You want **tight integration with Windows APIs.**

Choose PyQt if:

- You prefer **Python and want a native-feel UI.**
- You need a **lightweight, fast-performing application.**
- You are building a **customized UI-heavy application.**

3. Performance Considerations

3.1 Memory Usage

- **Electron apps are memory-intensive** because they embed a full web browser (Chromium).
- **PyQt and .NET MAUI** use system-native UI components, resulting in lower memory usage.
- **Optimize memory usage** by reducing unnecessary background processes.

3.2 CPU Performance

- **.NET MAUI and PyQt have better CPU efficiency** since they don't need a web engine.
- **Electron consumes CPU resources** due to rendering overhead.

Solution:

- Use **lazy loading** to defer resource-heavy operations.
- Optimize event loops and avoid CPU-intensive scripts.

3.3 Reducing App Size

- **Electron apps can be bloated (~50MB or more per install).**
- **PyQt and .NET MAUI apps are smaller (~10-20MB).**
- **Optimize your app by:**
  - Removing unused dependencies.
  - Compressing assets and images.
  - Using **tree-shaking** to remove dead code.

3.4 Cross-Platform UI Performance

- **Electron apps might not feel native** because they use web-based UI.
- **PyQt and .NET MAUI** provide a true native experience.
- **UI animations are smoother in native frameworks.**

Solution:

- Use **hardware acceleration** when rendering animations.
- Cache UI components to **prevent reloading**.

4. Summary

Packaging Options:

Language	Framework	Packaging Tool	Output Format	
Python	PyQt, Tkinter, Kivy	PyInstaller	`.exe,` `.deb`	`.app,`
C#	.NET MAUI	`dotnet publish`	`.msi,` `.deb`	`.dmg,`
JavaScript	Electron	Electron Packager	`.exe,` `.deb`	`.app,`

Electron is best for **web-based desktop applications**. **.NET MAUI** is best for **native Windows/macOS/Linux applications**.

PyQt is best for **lightweight, Python-powered GUI apps**.

Performance Optimization Checklist

- 🏆 **Choose a native framework** (PyQt, .NET MAUI) instead of a web-based one (Electron) for better performance.

- ↻ **Use efficient memory management techniques** to reduce RAM usage.

- 🎨 **Optimize UI elements** for responsiveness and native look.

159

- **Reduce unnecessary dependencies** to minimize app size.

What's Next?

In the next chapter, we'll explore **microservices and API development**, including **how Python (FastAPI, Flask) and C# (ASP.NET Core) enable scalable backend systems**!

CHAPTER 13

MICROSERVICES AND API DEVELOPMENT

Microservices architecture is widely used in modern software development, allowing applications to be **scalable, modular, and maintainable**. Instead of building **monolithic** applications, microservices break an application into **smaller, independent services** that communicate through APIs.

In this chapter, we'll explore: **Why microservices? Building REST APIs in Python using FastAPI and Flask Creating APIs in C# using .NET Core Web API Connecting Python and C# services**

1. Why Microservices?

A **monolithic application** is a single, tightly coupled codebase where all components are interconnected. As the application grows, it becomes difficult to **scale, maintain, and deploy updates**.

Microservices architecture solves these issues by breaking the application into **independent services** that communicate through APIs.

Benefits of Microservices

Scalability – Services can be scaled independently (e.g., scale a payments service separately from a user authentication service).

Fault Isolation – A failure in one microservice does not crash the entire application.

Technology Flexibility – Different services can use **different programming languages** (e.g., **Python for data processing, C# for enterprise applications**).

Faster Development – Teams can work on separate microservices in parallel.

Easier Deployment – Each service can be deployed and updated independently.

Example of a Microservices-Based Application

Service	Technology
User Authentication	Python (Flask)
Product Catalog	C# (.NET Core)
Payments Processing	Python (FastAPI)
Notifications	Node.js

Each microservice **exposes REST APIs** that other services can consume.

---

2. Building REST APIs in Python (FastAPI, Flask)

Python is widely used for building **lightweight and high-performance REST APIs**. Two popular frameworks are **Flask** and **FastAPI**.

2.1 Creating a REST API with Flask

Flask is a **lightweight framework** for building APIs quickly.

163

Installation:

```sh
pip install flask
```

Example: Flask API

```python
from flask import Flask, jsonify, request

app = Flask(__name__)

@app.route("/api/greet", methods=["GET"])
def greet():
    return jsonify({"message": "Hello from Flask!"})

if __name__ == "__main__":
    app.run(port=5000)
```

Run the API:

```sh
python app.py
```

Test the API using cURL:

164

sh

```
curl http://127.0.0.1:5000/api/greet
```

Flask is great for small-scale APIs but lacks built-in async support.

2.2 Creating a REST API with FastAPI

FastAPI is a modern API framework with built-in **asynchronous support**.

Installation:

sh

```
pip install fastapi uvicorn
```

Example: FastAPI API

python

```
from fastapi import FastAPI

app = FastAPI()

@app.get("/api/greet")
```

165

```
async def greet():
    return {"message": "Hello from FastAPI!"}

if __name__ == "__main__":
    import uvicorn
    uvicorn.run(app,          host="127.0.0.1",
port=5001)
```

Run the API:

```sh
sh
```

```
uvicorn main:app --reload
```

FastAPI provides automatic documentation:

- Open **Swagger UI**: http://127.0.0.1:5001/docs
- Open **ReDoc**: http://127.0.0.1:5001/redoc

FastAPI is recommended for large-scale, high-performance APIs due to async support.

---

3. Creating APIs in C# (.NET Core Web API)

C# and **ASP.NET Core** are widely used for **enterprise-grade REST APIs**.

166

Create a new Web API project:

sh

```
dotnet new webapi -n MyWebApi
cd MyWebApi
```

Modify `Controllers/HelloController.cs`

csharp

```csharp
using Microsoft.AspNetCore.Mvc;

[ApiController]
[Route("api/greet")]
public class HelloController : ControllerBase
{
    [HttpGet]
    public IActionResult Get()
    {
        return Ok(new { message = "Hello from ASP.NET Core API!" });
    }
}
```

Run the API:

sh

```
dotnet run
```

Test using cURL:

```sh
sh
```

```sh
curl http://localhost:5000/api/greet
```

ASP.NET Core is best for high-performance, secure APIs used in enterprise applications.

---

4. Connecting Python and C# Microservices

Python and C# services can communicate **via REST APIs** or **message brokers (e.g., RabbitMQ, Kafka).**

4.1 Python Calling a C# API

If we have a **C# API running on** `http://localhost:5000/api/greet`, a Python service can call it:

```python
python

import requests

response                                  =
requests.get("http://localhost:5000/api/greet")
```

168

```
print(response.json())    # Output: {'message':
'Hello from ASP.NET Core API!'}
```

Python can easily call .NET APIs using `requests`.

4.2 C# Calling a Python API

If we have a **Python API running on** `http://localhost:5001/api/greet`, a C# service can call it:

```csharp
using System;
using System.Net.Http;
using System.Threading.Tasks;

class Program
{
    static async Task Main()
    {
        using HttpClient client = new
HttpClient();
        HttpResponseMessage response = await
client.GetAsync("http://localhost:5001/api/gree
t");
```

```
string          result          =          await
response.Content.ReadAsStringAsync();
      Console.WriteLine(result);
   }
}
```

C# can consume Python REST APIs using `HttpClient`.

4.3 Using Message Brokers for Communication

Instead of calling APIs directly, microservices can **send messages** using RabbitMQ, Kafka, or Redis.

Python Service Sending a Message (RabbitMQ)

```python
python

import pika

connection                                    =
pika.BlockingConnection(pika.ConnectionParamete
rs("localhost"))
channel = connection.channel()
channel.queue_declare(queue="task_queue")
```

```
channel.basic_publish(exchange="",
routing_key="task_queue",    body="Hello    from
Python!")
connection.close()
```

C# Service Receiving a Message

csharp

```csharp
using RabbitMQ.Client;
using RabbitMQ.Client.Events;
using System;
using System.Text;

class Program
{
    static void Main()
    {
        var factory = new ConnectionFactory() {
HostName = "localhost" };
        using var connection =
factory.CreateConnection();
        using var channel =
connection.CreateModel();

        channel.QueueDeclare(queue:
"task_queue");

        var consumer = new
EventingBasicConsumer(channel);
```

171

```
consumer.Received += (model, ea) =>
{
    var body = ea.Body.ToArray();
    var              message              =
Encoding.UTF8.GetString(body);
    Console.WriteLine($"Received:
{message}");
    };

    channel.BasicConsume(queue:
"task_queue",    autoAck:    true,    consumer:
consumer);
    Console.ReadLine();
    }
}
```

Message queues decouple microservices and improve reliability.

---

5. Summary

- **Microservices break applications into smaller, scalable services.**
- **Python (Flask, FastAPI) is great for lightweight APIs.**
- **C# (.NET Core Web API) is best for enterprise-grade APIs.**

172

- **Python and C# services communicate via REST APIs or message queues (RabbitMQ, Kafka).**
- **FastAPI is ideal for high-performance async APIs,** while **Flask is simpler for smaller services.**

What's Next?

In the next chapter, we'll explore **cloud computing and serverless solutions**, including **how to deploy Python and C# microservices on AWS, Azure, and Google Cloud**!

CHAPTER 14

CLOUD COMPUTING & SERVERLESS SOLUTIONS

Cloud computing allows developers to deploy applications that are **scalable, highly available, and cost-effective**. Python and C# applications can be deployed on cloud platforms such as **AWS, Azure, and Google Cloud**, and they can leverage **serverless computing** to run code without managing infrastructure.

In this chapter, we'll explore:
Deploying Python and C# applications on AWS, Azure, and Google Cloud
Serverless computing with AWS Lambda and Azure Functions
CI/CD pipelines for cloud-based cross-platform applications

1. Deploying Python and C# Applications on AWS, Azure, and Google Cloud

Different cloud providers offer various hosting solutions for **web applications, APIs, and microservices.**

1.1 Deploying Python Applications

Python applications can be hosted using **virtual machines, serverless functions, or containers.**

Hosting Python Web Apps on AWS (Elastic Beanstalk)
Install AWS CLI and Elastic Beanstalk CLI:

```sh
```

```sh
pip install awsebcli --upgrade
```

Initialize a Python application:

```sh
```

```sh
eb init -p python-3.8 my-python-app
```

Deploy the application:

```sh
```

```
eb create my-env
```

AWS Elastic Beanstalk automatically provisions and manages servers.

Hosting Python APIs on Google Cloud (App Engine)
Install Google Cloud SDK:

```sh
```

```
gcloud init
```

Create an `app.yaml` file:

```yaml
```

```
runtime: python39
entrypoint: gunicorn -b :$PORT main:app
```

Deploy the application:

```sh
```

```
gcloud app deploy
```

Google App Engine provides a **fully managed platform** for Python apps.

1.2 Deploying C# Applications

C# applications are best deployed using **Azure App Services, AWS Elastic Beanstalk, or Google Cloud Run**.

Deploying ASP.NET Core on Azure App Service Install Azure CLI:

```sh
az login
```

Create an App Service:

```sh
az webapp create --resource-group MyResourceGroup --plan MyPlan --name MyAspNetApp --runtime DOTNETCORE:6.0
```

Deploy the application:

```sh
dotnet publish -c Release
az webapp deploy --name MyAspNetApp --src-path ./bin/Release/net6.0/publish
```

177

Azure App Service automatically handles scaling and deployments.

Deploying C# APIs on AWS Lambda with API Gateway

Install AWS CLI and .NET Lambda tools:

```sh

dotnet tool install -g Amazon.Lambda.Tools
```

Create a Lambda function:

```sh

dotnet new lambda.AspNetCoreMinimalAPI -n MyLambdaApp
```

Deploy the function:

```sh

dotnet lambda deploy-function MyLambdaApp
```

AWS Lambda runs **serverless** without provisioning virtual machines.

---

2. Serverless Computing with AWS Lambda & Azure Functions

Serverless computing allows applications to **execute code on demand without provisioning servers**.

2.1 Python in AWS Lambda

AWS Lambda runs Python functions **without managing servers**.

Create a Python Lambda function (`lambda_function.py`)

python

```python
import json

def lambda_handler(event, context):
    return {
        "statusCode": 200,
        "body": json.dumps({"message": "Hello from AWS Lambda!"})
    }
```

Deploy the function

sh

```
aws    lambda    create-function    --function-name
MyPythonLambda \
    --runtime python3.9 \
    --role
arn:aws:iam::123456789012:role/lambda-role \
    --handler lambda_function.lambda_handler \
    --zip-file fileb://function.zip
```

AWS Lambda **automatically scales** and only runs when invoked.

2.2 C# in Azure Functions

Azure Functions allow **serverless execution of C# applications**.

Create an Azure Function

```sh
```

```
az    functionapp    create    --resource-group
MyResourceGroup --name MyFunctionApp --storage-
account mystorage --runtime dotnet
```

Example C# Function

```csharp
public static class HelloFunction
{
    [FunctionName("HelloFunction")]
    public static IActionResult Run(

[HttpTrigger(AuthorizationLevel.Function,
"get")] HttpRequest req,
        ILogger log)
    {
        return new OkObjectResult("Hello from
Azure Functions!");
    }
}
```

Azure Functions automatically execute **when triggered by an event**.

---

3. CI/CD Pipelines for Cloud-Based Cross-Platform Apps

CI/CD (Continuous Integration & Continuous Deployment) automates the process of **testing and deploying** applications.

3.1 CI/CD with GitHub Actions

GitHub Actions can **automate deployments to AWS, Azure, or Google Cloud**.

Example: Deploying a Python App to AWS Create `.github/workflows/deploy.yml`:

yaml

```
name: Deploy to AWS
on:
  push:
    branches:
      - main
jobs:
  deploy:
    runs-on: ubuntu-latest
    steps:
      - uses: actions/checkout@v2
      - name: Deploy to Elastic Beanstalk
        run: |
          pip install awsebcli
          eb deploy
```

Every push to `main` deploys the Python app to AWS.

3.2 CI/CD with Azure DevOps

Azure DevOps can be used to deploy **C# applications to Azure App Services**.

Example: Deploying ASP.NET Core App

```yaml
yaml

trigger:
- main

pool:
  vmImage: 'ubuntu-latest'

steps:
- task: UseDotNet@2
  inputs:
    packageType: 'sdk'
    version: '6.0.x'

- script: dotnet publish -c Release -o $(Build.ArtifactStagingDirectory)

- task: AzureWebApp@1
  inputs:
    azureSubscription: 'AzureSubscription'
    appName: 'MyAspNetApp'
    package: '$(Build.ArtifactStagingDirectory)/*.zip'
```

This pipeline builds and deploys a C# application to Azure.

---

4. Summary

Cloud Service	Python	C#
AWS Elastic Beanstalk	Django, Flask, FastAPI	ASP.NET Core
Azure App Service	Flask, FastAPI	ASP.NET Core
Google App Engine	Flask, Django	.NET Core
AWS Lambda (Serverless)	Python functions	.NET 6+
Azure Functions (Serverless)	Python functions	.NET 6+

AWS is best for scalable and serverless applications. Azure is ideal for enterprise applications and Microsoft-based workloads. Google Cloud is great for automatic scaling and AI-powered applications.

What's Next?

In the next chapter, we'll explore **performance optimization for cross-platform apps**, covering **profiling, debugging, and best practices for improving execution speed!**

PART 5

ADVANCED TECHNIQUES AND PERFORMANCE OPTIMIZATION

CHAPTER 15

PERFORMANCE OPTIMIZATION FOR CROSS-PLATFORM APPS

As applications grow in size and complexity, optimizing performance becomes critical, especially for cross-platform applications that need to work efficiently across multiple operating systems. This chapter focuses on profiling, debugging, memory management, and **multi-threading and asynchronous programming** to optimize performance.

In this chapter, we'll explore:
Profiling and debugging Python & C# applications
Memory management differences between Python and C#
Using multi-threading and async programming for efficiency

1. Profiling and Debugging Python & C# Applications

Profiling and debugging are essential for identifying performance bottlenecks, memory leaks, and areas where optimizations are needed.

1.1 Profiling Python Applications

Python provides several tools to **profile performance** and understand where your application spends time during execution.

Using cProfile for Profiling Python Code

`cProfile` is a built-in Python module for profiling the performance of Python programs.

Usage:

```sh
sh
```

```
python -m cProfile myscript.py
```

Example: Profiling a Function

```python
python

import cProfile
```

```
def slow_function():
    total = 0
    for i in range(1000000):
        total += i
    return total


cProfile.run('slow_function()')
```

This will display how much time was spent on each function call, helping identify slow parts of the code.

Using Py-Spy for Profiling Python

`Py-Spy` is an external tool to profile running Python applications without modifying the source code.

Installation:

sh

```
pip install py-spy
```

Usage:

sh

```
py-spy top --pid <PID>
```

189

It helps you visualize CPU usage, function calls, and identify slow processes in real-time.

1.2 Profiling C# Applications

.NET Core provides **built-in tools** for profiling C# applications, and there are external tools like **BenchmarkDotNet** for high-precision benchmarking.

Using Visual Studio Profiler

Visual Studio has a **Profiler** built-in that lets you profile CPU usage, memory allocation, and thread activity.

How to Use:

1. Open the application in **Visual Studio**.
2. Go to **Debug > Performance Profiler**.
3. Select the areas you want to profile (CPU usage, memory usage, etc.).

Using BenchmarkDotNet for C# Performance

`BenchmarkDotNet` is a library for benchmarking C# code.

Installation:

```sh
sh

dotnet add package BenchmarkDotNet
```

Example: Using BenchmarkDotNet to Measure Code Performance

```csharp
csharp

using BenchmarkDotNet.Attributes;
using BenchmarkDotNet.Running;

public class BenchmarkExample
{
    [Benchmark]
    public void TestMethod()
    {
        var total = 0;
        for (int i = 0; i < 1000000; i++)
        {
            total += i;
        }
    }
}

public class Program
{
    public static void Main(string[] args)
    {
```

191

```
    var              summary           =
BenchmarkRunner.Run<BenchmarkExample>();
    }
}
```

BenchmarkDotNet provides accurate performance metrics for identifying and optimizing code performance.

---

2. Memory Management Differences

Python and C# handle **memory management** differently, and understanding these differences is important for optimizing performance.

2.1 Python Memory Management

Python uses **automatic memory management** via **reference counting** and **garbage collection**.

Reference Counting

Python tracks the number of references to an object. When the reference count drops to zero, the object is deleted.

192

Garbage Collection

Python uses a **cyclic garbage collector** to clean up objects involved in reference cycles (e.g., circular references).

Monitoring Memory Usage in Python: Use the `sys` **module** and `gc` **module** to track memory usage.

```python
import sys
import gc

gc.collect()        # Manually trigger garbage collection
print(sys.getsizeof(object))  # Print the size of an object
```

Memory Optimization Tips for Python

- **Minimize object creation** in loops.
- Use `del` to remove references to large objects when they are no longer needed.
- Optimize large data structures by using **generators** instead of lists.

2.2 C# Memory Management

C# uses **automatic memory management** with **garbage collection** and **managed heaps**.

Garbage Collection in C#

C#'s **garbage collector** handles memory management by automatically reclaiming memory from unused objects. The garbage collector runs in the background and periodically frees memory from **unreachable objects**.

Memory Management Tips for C#

- Use `Dispose()` for objects that manage **unmanaged resources** (e.g., file streams, database connections).
- **Minimize object allocations** to reduce the pressure on the garbage collector.
- Use **memory pools** to reuse memory instead of allocating new memory objects frequently.

Example: Using `Dispose()` to Free Resources in C#

csharp

```
using (var stream = new FileStream("file.txt",
FileMode.Open))
{
    // Use the stream
```

```
}  // The FileStream is automatically disposed of
here.
```

---

3. Using Multi-Threading and Async Programming for Efficiency

Efficient multi-threading and asynchronous programming can significantly improve performance by making better use of CPU resources and allowing non-blocking I/O operations.

3.1 Multi-Threading in Python

Python supports **multi-threading**, but due to the **Global Interpreter Lock (GIL)**, it doesn't fully utilize multi-core CPUs for CPU-bound tasks.

Using `threading` for I/O-bound Operations
```python
python

import threading

def worker():
    print("Worker thread started")

# Create and start multiple threads
threads = []
for _ in range(5):
```

195

```
thread = threading.Thread(target=worker)
thread.start()
threads.append(thread)

# Wait for all threads to complete
for thread in threads:
    thread.join()
```

Using `concurrent.futures` for Thread Pooling

For better performance, use **ThreadPoolExecutor** to manage a pool of threads.

```python
python

from concurrent.futures import ThreadPoolExecutor

def task(n):
    print(f"Task {n} started")

with ThreadPoolExecutor(max_workers=5) as executor:
    for i in range(5):
        executor.submit(task, i)
```

3.2 Async Programming in Python

For **I/O-bound tasks** (e.g., file reading, HTTP requests), Python's `asyncio` allows for **non-blocking** code execution.

Async Example with `asyncio`

python

```python
import asyncio

async def fetch_data():
    print("Fetching data...")
    await asyncio.sleep(2)
    print("Data fetched")

# Run the async function
asyncio.run(fetch_data())
```

`asyncio` enables efficient **I/O-bound operations**, allowing the program to handle other tasks while waiting for I/O operations.

3.3 Multi-Threading in C#

C# allows **true multi-threading** with the **Task Parallel Library (TPL)** and **Thread class**, making it effective for **CPU-bound operations**.

Using `Task` for Asynchronous Programming

csharp

```
using System;
using System.Threading.Tasks;

public class Program
{
    public static async Task Main(string[] args)
    {
        await    Task.WhenAll(FetchDataAsync(),
FetchDataAsync());
    }

    static async Task FetchDataAsync()
    {
        Console.WriteLine("Fetching data...");
        await Task.Delay(2000);
        Console.WriteLine("Data fetched");
    }
}
```

`Task` provides asynchronous functionality, enabling **non-blocking execution** in C#.

Using `Parallel.For` for Multi-Threading

csharp

```
using System;
```

```
using System.Threading.Tasks;

public class Program
{
    public static void Main(string[] args)
    {
        Parallel.For(0, 5, i =>
        {
            Console.WriteLine($"Task        {i}
started");
        });
    }
}
```

Parallelism allows multi-core processors to execute multiple threads simultaneously, improving performance for **CPU-bound tasks**.

---

4. Summary

- **Profiling and Debugging:** Use **cProfile** (Python) and **Visual Studio Profiler** (C#) to identify performance bottlenecks.
- **Memory Management:**
  - **Python** uses **reference counting and garbage collection**.

199

- o C# uses **garbage collection** and manual memory management for unmanaged resources.
- **Multi-Threading & Async Programming:**
  - o **Python** supports **multi-threading** for I/O-bound tasks and **asyncio** for efficient I/O.
  - o **C#** uses **Task Parallel Library (TPL)** and **async/await** for both I/O and CPU-bound tasks.

What's Next?

In the next chapter, we'll explore **security best practices** for cross-platform apps, covering **data encryption, authentication, and securing APIs**!

CHAPTER 16

SECURITY BEST PRACTICES IN CROSS-PLATFORM DEVELOPMENT

Security is a critical aspect of any application, particularly cross-platform applications that run on various operating systems and devices. Protecting data, ensuring privacy, and preventing common vulnerabilities are essential for building secure applications.

In this chapter, we'll explore: **Securing web apps, APIs, and desktop software Preventing common vulnerabilities Implementing authentication and authorization across platforms**

1. Securing Web Apps, APIs, and Desktop Software

Security practices vary depending on the type of application. Below, we discuss securing **web applications**, **APIs**, and **desktop applications**.

1.1 Securing Web Apps

Web apps often face a variety of attacks from external sources. Protecting web apps requires careful handling of **user input**, **session management**, and **data encryption**.

Common Web Security Best Practices:

1. **Use   HTTPS**
   Always serve your web app over **HTTPS** (SSL/TLS) to encrypt data in transit and protect against **man-in-the-middle attacks**.

2. **Sanitize   User   Input**
   Never trust user input directly. Always **sanitize and validate** input to protect against **SQL Injection, XSS (Cross-Site Scripting)**, and **Command Injection**.
   - Use **prepared statements** or **ORM frameworks** to prevent SQL Injection.

202

o **Escape special characters** in user inputs to avoid XSS.

3. **Cross-Site Request Forgery (CSRF) Protection**
Protect your web apps from **CSRF** attacks by using **anti-CSRF tokens** in form submissions and AJAX requests.

4. **Content Security Policy (CSP)**
Implement **CSP headers** to restrict what content can be loaded on your site, preventing XSS attacks.

5. **Session Management**
o Use **secure, HttpOnly, and SameSite cookies** to store session tokens.

o **Implement session expiration** and **invalidate sessions** after a period of inactivity.

6. **Rate Limiting and Logging**
Use **rate limiting** to prevent brute-force attacks and keep detailed **logs** for detecting suspicious activity.

1.2 Securing APIs

APIs are often the backbone of modern applications, and securing them is crucial.

Common API Security Best Practices:

1. **Use OAuth2 and JWT for Authentication**
   Implement **OAuth2** with **JWT (JSON Web Tokens)** for **token-based authentication**. This ensures that users' credentials are not stored on the server, reducing the risk of credential theft.

2. **API Rate Limiting**
   Protect APIs from **denial-of-service (DoS)** attacks by implementing **rate limiting** and **IP blacklisting**.

3. **Input Validation**
   Validate incoming data in APIs to protect against **injection attacks**. Use libraries like **Joi (Node.js)** or **Cerberus (Python)** to validate the structure and data types of the input.

4. **CORS (Cross-Origin Resource Sharing) Policies**
   Implement **CORS** to control which domains can access your API and prevent unauthorized access.

5. **Use API Keys and Secrets**
   Require **API keys** for external clients to interact with your API. Keep keys and secrets in **environment variables** or secret management systems, never hard-code them in the source code.

6. **Secure Communication**
   Always use **HTTPS** to encrypt data sent over the

204

network. Never transmit sensitive data over unencrypted channels.

1.3 Securing Desktop Software

While desktop applications are not exposed to the web directly, they are still vulnerable to **local attacks**, and securing them is equally important.

Common Desktop Security Best Practices:

1. **Data   Encryption**
   Encrypt sensitive data (e.g., passwords, personal information) **at rest** and **in transit** using **AES-256** or similar encryption algorithms. Use **public key infrastructure (PKI)** for key management.

2. **Secure File Handling**
   o   Ensure that **file paths** provided by the user are validated to prevent directory traversal attacks.
   o   **Use sandboxing** for untrusted code execution to prevent malware from accessing system resources.

3. **Code   Obfuscation**
   Use **code obfuscation** techniques to prevent reverse

engineering of your desktop software and to protect intellectual property.

4. **Update**   **Mechanisms**

   Implement an **auto-update system** that ensures the application remains up-to-date with the latest security patches.

---

2. Preventing Common Vulnerabilities

Cross-platform applications are susceptible to many common vulnerabilities, such as **SQL injection, XSS**, and **buffer overflows**. Here's how to prevent these threats.

2.1 SQL Injection

SQL Injection occurs when untrusted input is used in SQL queries, allowing attackers to manipulate the query.

Prevent SQL Injection:

- **Use parameterized queries** (prepared statements) instead of string concatenation.
- In **Python**, use **SQLAlchemy** or **Django ORM**, which prevent SQL injection.

- In **C#**, use **Entity Framework** or **ADO.NET** parameterized queries.

Example: C# using Entity Framework

```csharp
var query = context.Users.Where(u => u.Username
== username && u.Password == password);
```

Example: Python using SQLAlchemy

```python
result = db.session.execute("SELECT * FROM users
WHERE username = :username", {'username':
username})
```

2.2 Cross-Site Scripting (XSS)

XSS occurs when attackers inject malicious scripts into web pages viewed by others, potentially stealing data from users.

Prevent XSS:

- **Sanitize user input** to remove any HTML or JavaScript code.

- **Escape data** using encoding functions (`html.escape()` in Python or `HttpUtility.HtmlEncode()` in C#).
- Use **Content Security Policy (CSP)** to restrict the types of content that can be executed on a page.

2.3 Cross-Site Request Forgery (CSRF)

CSRF attacks occur when an attacker tricks a user into performing unwanted actions on a web application where the user is authenticated.

Prevent CSRF:

- Use **anti-CSRF tokens** in every form submission and AJAX request.
- Ensure the **SameSite** attribute is set on cookies, which prevents cross-site requests from being sent automatically.

2.4 Buffer Overflows

A **buffer overflow** occurs when a program writes more data to a buffer than it can hold, potentially allowing attackers to execute arbitrary code.

Prevent Buffer Overflows:

- Use **safe functions** (e.g., `strncpy` in C, or **safe string libraries**).
- In **C#**, use **managed code** (like arrays and strings), which are protected from buffer overflows.

3. Implementing Authentication & Authorization Across Platforms

Authentication and authorization are core components of any secure application, ensuring that only authorized users can access specific resources.

3.1 Authentication:

Authentication verifies the identity of a user. Common methods include **username/password, OAuth**, and **multi-factor authentication (MFA)**.

- **Use OAuth 2.0** with **JWT** tokens for **stateless authentication**.
- **Enable MFA** (SMS, email, or authenticator apps) for higher security.
- Implement **social logins** (Google, Facebook) for convenience and security.

3.2 Authorization:

Authorization ensures users can only access resources they are permitted to. Common strategies include **role-based access control (RBAC)** and **attribute-based access control (ABAC)**.

- **RBAC**: Assign roles (e.g., Admin, User) and grant permissions based on roles.
- **ABAC**: Use attributes (e.g., user's department or clearance level) to grant access to resources.

Example: C# Authorization with Roles

```
csharp

public class MyController : Controller
{
    [Authorize(Roles = "Admin")]
    public IActionResult AdminPanel()
    {
        return View();
```

210

```
    }
}
```

Example: Python Flask Authorization

```python
from flask import Flask, request, jsonify

@app.route('/admin')
@requires_roles('admin')
def admin():
    return jsonify(message="Welcome to the admin
panel")
```

4. Summary

- **Securing web apps**: Use HTTPS, validate user input, protect against CSRF and XSS.
- **Securing APIs**: Implement OAuth2, rate limiting, and secure communication via HTTPS.
- **Securing desktop apps**: Encrypt data, handle files securely, and use code obfuscation.
- **Preventing vulnerabilities**: Address common issues like **SQL injection, XSS**, and **buffer overflows** with appropriate coding practices.
- **Authentication and Authorization**: Implement secure login (OAuth2, JWT), enforce roles, and use MFA for added security.

What's Next?

In the next chapter, we'll explore **cloud-native app development**, including **how to leverage cloud services like Kubernetes and Docker for cross-platform applications**!

CHAPTER 17

TESTING AND DEBUGGING CROSS-PLATFORM APPLICATIONS

Effective **testing** and **debugging** are essential for ensuring that cross-platform applications work correctly and efficiently across all target systems. Python and C# provide robust frameworks for unit testing, and both languages offer powerful tools for debugging and troubleshooting.

In this chapter, we'll explore:
Unit testing in Python (pytest, unittest)
Unit testing in C# (NUnit, xUnit)
Cross-platform debugging techniques

---

1. Unit Testing in Python (pytest, unittest)

Unit testing ensures that individual components of your code (functions, methods, classes) work as expected. Python provides multiple testing frameworks, with **unittest** (built-in) and **pytest** (third-party) being the most popular.

1.1 Unit Testing with unittest (Built-in Python)

Python's **unittest** module follows the **xUnit** style for defining test cases. It is part of the Python standard library.

Basic Example of unit tests with unittest

python

```
import unittest

def add(a, b):
    return a + b

class TestAddFunction(unittest.TestCase):
    def test_add(self):
        self.assertEqual(add(2, 3), 5)
        self.assertEqual(add(-1, 1), 0)
        self.assertEqual(add(-1, -1), -2)

if __name__ == '__main__':
    unittest.main()
```

Run the tests using:

sh

```
python -m unittest test_script.py
```

Key features of unittest:

- Supports **test discovery**.
- **Assertions** like `assertEqual()`, `assertNotEqual()`, `assertTrue()`.
- Built-in support for **test fixtures** (e.g., `setUp()` and `tearDown()`).

1.2 Unit Testing with pytest (Third-Party Python)

pytest is a popular testing framework due to its simplicity, flexibility, and extensive feature set.

Installation:

sh

```
pip install pytest
```

Basic Example of unit tests with pytest

python

```
def add(a, b):
    return a + b

def test_add():
    assert add(2, 3) == 5
```

215

```
assert add(-1, 1) == 0
assert add(-1, -1) == -2
```

Run the tests using:

sh

```
pytest test_script.py
```

Key features of pytest:

- **Auto-discovery** of tests.
- Powerful **assertion rewriting** (you can use simple `assert` statements).
- Support for **fixtures** (e.g., database setup) and **parameterized tests**.

---

2. Unit Testing in C# (NUnit, xUnit)

In C#, **NUnit** and **xUnit** are the most popular frameworks for unit testing. These frameworks allow for writing tests that help ensure code correctness across different platforms.

2.1 Unit Testing with NUnit

NUnit is a mature unit testing framework for .NET, inspired by JUnit.

216

Installation:

1. Install NUnit via NuGet:

sh

```
dotnet add package NUnit
dotnet add package NUnit3TestAdapter
dotnet add package Microsoft.NET.Test.Sdk
```

Basic Example of NUnit Test

csharp

```csharp
using NUnit.Framework;

public class TestAddFunction
{
    [Test]
    public void TestAdd()
    {
        Assert.AreEqual(5, Add(2, 3));
        Assert.AreEqual(0, Add(-1, 1));
        Assert.AreEqual(-2, Add(-1, -1));
    }

    public int Add(int a, int b)
    {
        return a + b;
    }
}
```

Run the tests:

```sh
sh
```

```
dotnet test
```

Key features of NUnit:

- Supports **data-driven tests** using attributes like `[TestCase]`.
- Advanced **assertion methods** such as `Assert.AreEqual()`, `Assert.IsTrue()`, `Assert.IsNotNull()`.
- Integration with **Visual Studio** and **CI/CD pipelines**.

2.2 Unit Testing with xUnit

xUnit is a newer, **lightweight testing framework** for .NET that is community-driven and widely adopted in modern C# applications.

Installation:

1. Install xUnit via NuGet:

```sh
sh
```

218

```
dotnet add package xUnit
dotnet add package xunit.runner.visualstudio
dotnet add package Microsoft.NET.Test.Sdk
```

Basic Example of xUnit Test

```csharp
using Xunit;

public class TestAddFunction
{
    [Fact]
    public void TestAdd()
    {
        Assert.Equal(5, Add(2, 3));
        Assert.Equal(0, Add(-1, 1));
        Assert.Equal(-2, Add(-1, -1));
    }

    public int Add(int a, int b)
    {
        return a + b;
    }
}
```

Run the tests:

```sh
dotnet test
```

Key features of xUnit:

- Simple and **lightweight** design.
- **Fact and Theory attributes** for simple and parameterized tests.
- Great integration with **CI/CD pipelines** and **Visual Studio**.

3. Cross-Platform Debugging Techniques

Debugging cross-platform applications requires understanding platform-specific tools and general debugging strategies to troubleshoot issues effectively across **Windows, macOS, and Linux**.

3.1 Debugging Python Applications

Using the Built-in Python Debugger (pdb)

`pdb` is Python's built-in debugger, and it allows you to set breakpoints and inspect the program's state during execution.

Example: Debugging with `pdb`

```
python
```

```
import pdb

def add(a, b):
    pdb.set_trace()    # Set a breakpoint here
    return a + b

add(2, 3)
```

Run the program:

```sh
```

```
python -m pdb myscript.py
```

Using PyCharm Debugger

PyCharm offers an advanced **visual debugger** that works cross-platform (Windows, macOS, and Linux). It supports **breakpoints**, **step-through debugging**, **watches**, and **variable inspection**.

3.2 Debugging C# Applications

Using Visual Studio Debugger

Visual Studio provides a powerful debugger that supports **cross-platform debugging** for **.NET Core apps** running on Windows, macOS, and Linux.

Key Features:

- **Breakpoints** and **watch windows** for inspecting variables.
- **Step-through** and **step-over** capabilities.
- **Cross-platform debugging** with **remote debugging** on Linux and macOS.

Using Visual Studio Code Debugger

VS Code with the **C# extension** can be used to debug **.NET Core** applications on all major platforms.

Launch Configuration (launch.json):

json

```json
{
  "version": "0.2.0",
  "configurations": [
    {
      "name": ".NET Core Launch (web)",
```

```
      "type": "coreclr",
      "request": "launch",
      "program":
"${workspaceFolder}/bin/Debug/netcoreapp3.1/MyA
pp.dll",
      "args": [],
      "cwd": "${workspaceFolder}",
      "stopAtEntry": false,
      "serverReadyAction": {
        "action": "openExternally",
        "pattern":        "\\bNow        listening
on:\\s+(https?://\\S+)"
      },
      "serverReadyTimeout": 5000,
      "sourceFileMap": {
        "/Views": "${workspaceFolder}/Views"
      }
    }
  ]
}
```

3.3 Remote Debugging for Cross-Platform Apps

Sometimes, you may need to debug a remote machine, especially when working with cloud services or Linux-based containers.

Remote Debugging in Python

- Use **PyCharm** or **VS Code** to connect to remote machines using **SSH**.
- Set up **remote Python interpreters** for remote debugging.

Remote Debugging in C#

- Visual Studio and **VS Code** can be used to **remotely debug** applications on Linux and macOS machines using **SSH**.
- **Docker containers** running .NET Core apps can be debugged using **Visual Studio Code** with the **Remote - Containers extension**.

---

4. Summary

- **Unit testing**: Use **unittest** or **pytest** in Python, and **NUnit** or **xUnit** in C# to test the individual components of your code.
- **Cross-platform debugging**: Use built-in tools like **pdb** in Python or advanced IDEs like **PyCharm** and **Visual Studio** for debugging.
- **Remote debugging**: Both Python and C# support remote debugging on different operating systems.

What's Next?

In the next chapter, we'll dive into **building scalable applications** using **microservices architecture** and explore best practices for handling **distributed systems** and **message brokers**.

PART 6

REAL-WORLD APPLICATIONS & FUTURE TRENDS

CHAPTER 18

CASE STUDIES: SUCCESSFUL CROSS-PLATFORM APPLICATIONS

Cross-platform development has become essential for companies aiming to reach a **broad user base** and streamline their development processes. Python and C# are two of the most popular languages used for building cross-platform applications, and many companies have successfully leveraged these technologies to create scalable, user-friendly software solutions.

In this chapter, we'll explore:
Real-world examples of software built with Python and C#
Lessons from companies using cross-platform approaches

1. Real-World Examples of Software Built with Python & C#

1.1 Python: Real-World Cross-Platform Applications

1.1.1 Dropbox (Python)

Dropbox is a widely used cloud storage service that was initially built using **Python** for the backend services and desktop application.

- **Key Technologies**: Python, SQLite, PyQt, and wxPython for desktop GUI.
- **Cross-Platform Challenge**: Dropbox had to ensure seamless functionality on **Windows, macOS**, and **Linux**. Python's **cross-platform capabilities** and **third-party libraries** made it easier for Dropbox to create a consistent experience across these operating systems.
- **Result**: Dropbox's desktop client works across all major platforms, including automatic syncing and file management.

Lessons Learned:

- **Cross-Platform Consistency**: Using Python's **PyQt** and **wxPython** ensured that Dropbox maintained a **consistent**

UI across platforms without rewriting the GUI for each OS.

- **Leverage open-source libraries**: Python's extensive ecosystem of libraries helped Dropbox achieve rapid development without needing to develop everything in-house.

1.1.2 Spotify (Python)

Spotify, the popular music streaming platform, uses **Python** for its backend services, particularly for handling data processing, recommendation algorithms, and user interactions.

- **Key Technologies**: Python for backend logic, with frameworks like **Django** and **Flask**.
- **Cross-Platform Challenge**: Spotify needed to scale its services to handle millions of users on **Windows**, **macOS**, **Linux**, and **mobile platforms**.
- **Result**: Python enabled Spotify to rapidly iterate on their services and create a **cross-platform experience** with **minimal code duplication**.

Lessons Learned:

- **Scalability**: Python's **asyncio** and **Celery** helped Spotify scale its backend to handle large numbers of concurrent users.
- **Flexibility**: The ability to leverage Python's vast library ecosystem meant Spotify could build custom features quickly and efficiently.

1.2 C#: Real-World Cross-Platform Applications

1.2.1 Microsoft Visual Studio Code (C#)

Visual Studio Code (VS Code), one of the most popular code editors globally, is built using **C#** and **Electron**. While the core editor is based on web technologies, C# plays a significant role in its performance and extension support.

- **Key Technologies**: C#, JavaScript, Electron, Node.js.
- **Cross-Platform Challenge**: Visual Studio Code needed to function well across **Windows**, **macOS**, and **Linux** while offering a seamless experience.
- **Result**: VS Code is one of the most widely used code editors due to its **performance, extensibility**, and **cross-platform compatibility**.

Lessons Learned:

- **Combining Technologies**: Visual Studio Code shows how combining **C#** (for performance) with **Electron** (for cross-platform UI) can lead to **robust cross-platform software**.

- **Performance and Extensibility**: C# was used for the underlying engine and performance optimizations, while Electron handled the UI.

1.2.2 JetBrains Rider (C#)

JetBrains Rider, an integrated development environment (IDE) for .NET development, uses **C#** and **IntelliJ Platform** for cross-platform support.

- **Key Technologies**: C#, Java, IntelliJ Platform.
- **Cross-Platform Challenge**: Rider needed to ensure that .NET developers had access to a **robust IDE** across **Windows, macOS**, and **Linux**.
- **Result**: Rider offers advanced **debugging, unit testing**, and **refactoring** features across all platforms, making it a top choice for **cross-platform .NET development**.

Lessons Learned:

- **UI and Backend Decoupling**: Rider uses **IntelliJ Platform** for its core IDE logic, but C# is used for platform-specific services and optimizations.
- **Optimizing Performance**: The team focused on **memory management** and **threading** in C# to ensure that the IDE is responsive on all platforms.

2. Lessons from Companies Using Cross-Platform Approaches

2.1 The Importance of Choosing the Right Framework

- **Cross-platform frameworks** like **Electron, .NET MAUI, Qt,** and **Xamarin** provide a **single codebase** to support multiple platforms, but **each framework has its trade-offs** in terms of performance, scalability, and UI/UX consistency.
  - o **Electron** is great for apps that need to leverage **web technologies** but can lead to **higher resource usage**.
  - o **.NET MAUI** is ideal for **native-like experiences** but requires familiarity with the **.NET ecosystem**.

232

- o **PyQt** offers **native desktop apps** with Python, but may not perform as well as fully native C# apps.

2.2 Optimizing User Experience Across Platforms

- Successful cross-platform apps, such as **Spotify** and **Visual Studio Code**, have invested heavily in **platform-specific optimizations**. Even though the core functionality is shared across platforms, these apps fine-tune the user experience for each operating system, ensuring the app **feels native** on every platform.
  - o **Key Consideration**: Pay attention to **UI consistency** across platforms while also providing a **native look and feel**.
  - o **Example**: Spotify uses **platform-specific UIs** (e.g., custom context menus on macOS) while keeping the core design consistent across **Windows** and **Linux**.

2.3 Leveraging Cloud and Backend for Scalability

- Many companies with cross-platform applications, such as **Dropbox** and **Spotify**, focus on **backend scalability** and **cloud-based infrastructure** to

233

ensure that their applications handle **large user bases** efficiently.

- o **Key Strategy**: Use cloud services like **AWS**, **Azure**, and **Google Cloud** to offload heavy tasks such as data storage, image processing, and machine learning, enabling cross-platform apps to remain responsive and scalable.

2.4 Continuous Integration and Deployment (CI/CD) for Cross-Platform Apps

- **Automating the build and deployment process** is crucial when maintaining a **cross-platform application**. Teams often use **CI/CD pipelines** to deploy software to **multiple platforms** (Windows, macOS, Linux) from a **single repository**.
  - o **Example**: **GitHub Actions** or **Azure DevOps** can automate the build, test, and deployment processes across platforms, ensuring that updates are pushed quickly and efficiently to users on all platforms.

234

3. Summary

- **Successful Python Cross-Platform Apps**: Dropbox, Spotify – built using Python's **extensive library ecosystem** and frameworks like **PyQt** for GUI development.
- **Successful C# Cross-Platform Apps**: Visual Studio Code, JetBrains Rider – leveraging **C# for performance** and **Electron for cross-platform UI**.
- **Key Lessons**:
  - **Choose the right framework** for your specific app needs.
  - Focus on **optimizing user experience** for each platform while maintaining a **consistent design**.
  - Use **cloud-based infrastructure** for **scalability** and **CI/CD pipelines** to streamline deployment.

What's Next?

In the next chapter, we'll look at **future trends in cross-platform development**, including **the rise of WebAssembly, progressive web apps (PWAs)**, and the evolution of **mobile frameworks** like **Flutter** and **React Native**.

CHAPTER 19

THE FUTURE OF CROSS-PLATFORM DEVELOPMENT

Cross-platform development has come a long way in enabling developers to create applications that work seamlessly across **Windows, macOS, Linux**, and **mobile platforms**. As technology continues to evolve, there are several **emerging trends** that are shaping the future of cross-platform development, including the increasing integration of **AI and machine learning**, and the rise of **Progressive Web Apps (PWAs)**.

In this chapter, we'll explore:
Emerging trends in Python and C# development
The impact of AI and machine learning on cross-platform **apps**
The rise of Progressive Web Apps (PWAs)

1. Emerging Trends in Python & C# Development

Both **Python** and **C#** continue to evolve and adapt to meet the demands of modern cross-platform development. Here are some emerging trends in the development of both languages:

1.1 Python Development Trends

1.1.1 Enhanced Support for Mobile Development

While Python has historically been limited in mobile development, frameworks like **BeeWare** and **Kivy** are improving, and new tools are emerging to make Python more effective for mobile apps.

- **BeeWare**: Allows developers to build **native desktop and mobile applications** from a single Python codebase, offering support for **iOS** and **Android**.
- **Kivy**: Continues to evolve as a framework for building **touch-based applications** for mobile devices, tablets, and desktops.

1.1.2 Python for Machine Learning and AI

Python's **dominance in AI and machine learning** is expected to continue. Libraries like **TensorFlow, Keras,**

PyTorch, and **Scikit-learn** will remain critical tools for **cross-platform AI applications**.

- Python's **data science ecosystem** will continue to be integrated into cross-platform apps, making it easier to incorporate **AI models** in applications that run on multiple platforms.

1.1.3 Cloud-Native Python Development

The future of Python is **cloud-native**, with Python playing a major role in developing **serverless functions**, microservices, and applications that run on platforms like **AWS Lambda** and **Google Cloud Functions**.

- Python's ease of use and integration with cloud platforms will make it a go-to choice for **cloud-based applications** and microservices in cross-platform development.

1.2 C# Development Trends

1.2.1 .NET MAUI and Cross-Platform Expansion

.NET MAUI (Multi-platform App UI) is set to be the successor of Xamarin, allowing **C# developers** to build

native desktop and mobile apps with a single codebase. .NET MAUI extends the capabilities of **Xamarin Forms** to include support for **Windows, macOS, Android**, and **iOS**.

- The **unification of the .NET ecosystem** under **.NET 6** and beyond is simplifying the development of cross-platform apps, making C# a central language for both **mobile and desktop** applications.

1.2.2 Blazor and WebAssembly

With **Blazor**, developers can now build **web applications** using **C#** instead of JavaScript. Blazor WebAssembly runs C# code directly in the browser, eliminating the need for JavaScript for frontend development.

- This trend is likely to grow, enabling **C# developers** to use **WebAssembly** for more powerful and **efficient cross-platform web apps** that run across devices, from desktop to mobile.

1.2.3 Cloud and DevOps with .NET

C# developers are increasingly leveraging **cloud platforms** such as **Azure** for building **cloud-native applications**. With **containerization** using **Docker** and orchestration with **Kubernetes**, C# and **.NET Core** are becoming key technologies for building scalable, secure, and performant cloud applications.

- Integration with **Azure Functions** and **Microservices** will continue to play a significant role in C#'s evolution for cross-platform, scalable cloud applications.

2. The Impact of AI and Machine Learning on Cross-Platform Apps

The integration of **artificial intelligence (AI)** and **machine learning (ML)** into cross-platform applications is becoming increasingly important as companies look to create **smarter applications** that can provide **personalized user experiences**, **predictive analytics**, and **automation**.

2.1 AI for Personalized User Experiences

AI-powered features like **recommendation systems** (used by apps like **Netflix**, **Spotify**, and **Amazon**) can be integrated into cross-platform apps built with Python and C#.

- **Python** continues to be the go-to language for AI, and its powerful machine learning libraries

240

(**TensorFlow**, **Keras**, **PyTorch**) will allow developers to build predictive models and **AI-enhanced features** into their cross-platform apps.

- **C#** can also leverage machine learning through **ML.NET** (Microsoft's open-source machine learning framework), which allows developers to build **cross-platform machine learning models** using C# and .NET.

2.2 AI for Automation and Efficiency

AI-driven automation can streamline various aspects of cross-platform development, such as **bug detection**, **testing**, and **CI/CD pipelines**.

- Python's integration with tools like **PyTest** and **Selenium** can be enhanced with AI to **automatically detect bugs** in different environments and **optimize performance**.
- **C# developers** can leverage **Azure AI services** like **Cognitive Services** to build AI-powered features such as **natural language processing (NLP)**, **image recognition**, and **speech-to-text**, making cross-platform apps more interactive and intelligent.

241

2.3 AI-Powered Cross-Platform Apps

AI can also enhance the **cross-platform functionality** by enabling applications to operate intelligently on different platforms.

- **Recommendation systems** can be built to personalize content, such as in **news apps** or **e-commerce platforms**.
- **Natural language processing** (NLP) can allow users to **interact with apps** via voice or chatbots.
- **Real-time data processing** and **image analysis** can be implemented in apps that require **cross-platform compatibility** for tasks like **healthcare analysis** and **image recognition**.

The integration of AI is driving **smarter cross-platform applications** with greater **performance** and **user engagement**.

3. The Rise of Progressive Web Apps (PWAs)

Progressive Web Apps (PWAs) are **web applications** that behave like native mobile apps but are accessible via the browser. They are becoming increasingly important in the cross-platform development landscape.

3.1 What are PWAs?

PWAs combine the best features of **web** and **mobile applications**:

- **Offline access**: PWAs can function offline or on low-quality networks.
- **App-like experience**: They offer a **native-like interface** with smooth animations and interactions.
- **No installation required**: PWAs can be added to the home screen directly from the browser, without needing to go through an app store.

3.2 Advantages of PWAs for Cross-Platform Development

- **Cross-Platform Compatibility**: PWAs can run on **any platform** (Windows, macOS, Linux, iOS, Android) as long as there is a browser, reducing the need for multiple app versions.
- **Reduced Development Costs**: Since PWAs are built using **web technologies** (HTML, CSS, JavaScript), companies do not need to build separate versions for different platforms.

243

- **Improved Performance**: PWAs are **lightweight**, **fast**, and support **service workers** to manage caching and background tasks, making them suitable for **low-latency applications**.

3.3 The Future of PWAs in Cross-Platform Development

As **browser capabilities** continue to improve, the adoption of **PWAs** will rise. Major platforms like **Chrome, Firefox**, and **Edge** now support PWAs, and mobile operating systems like **Android** allow users to install PWAs on their home screens.

- **WebAssembly (Wasm)** will enhance PWAs by enabling **high-performance computing** directly in the browser, making them more suitable for **graphic-intensive** applications like games and design tools.
- **C# with Blazor** is already paving the way for building **PWAs with C#**, allowing developers to write web apps using C# and deploy them as native-like apps across all platforms.

4. Summary

Emerging Trends in Cross-Platform Development:

- **Python and C#** are evolving to support **cloud-native**, **mobile**, and **AI-powered applications**.
- **AI and ML** are increasingly integrated into cross-platform apps, enhancing **personalized experiences**, **automation**, and **real-time data processing**.
- **Progressive Web Apps (PWAs)** offer a **unified solution** for building **cross-platform apps** that work seamlessly across all devices and platforms, reducing development costs and improving performance.

Future Outlook:

- **Cross-platform frameworks** like **.NET MAUI, Flutter**, and **React Native** will continue to shape the landscape of mobile app development.
- The rise of **WebAssembly** and **Blazor** will allow **web applications** to offer **native-like experiences** with C#.
- **AI and machine learning** will empower developers to create **smarter** and **more interactive cross-platform apps**.

What's Next?

In the final chapter, we'll conclude our journey with **best practices** for **building sustainable, scalable, and secure cross-platform applications**, and share insights into how the development landscape is evolving in the long term.

CHAPTER 20

BUILDING YOUR OWN CROSS-PLATFORM PROJECT

Building a cross-platform application can be a rewarding challenge, as it allows you to reach a **broad user base** across **Windows, macOS, Linux**, and **mobile platforms**. However, choosing the right **tech stack**, structuring your project properly, and following best practices are crucial to ensure that your project is efficient, maintainable, and scalable.

In this chapter, we'll explore:
Choosing the right tech stack
Best practices for structuring projects
Final tips and resources for continuous learning

---

1. Choosing the Right Tech Stack

The **tech stack** you choose for your cross-platform application will define the **architecture**, **scalability**, and

maintainability of your project. There are several important considerations when selecting the right tech stack:

1.1 Key Factors in Choosing a Tech Stack

- **Project Requirements**: What features does the application need? Is it more focused on **data processing**, **UI/UX**, or **performance**? Make sure to choose tools that are well-suited for the project's specific needs.
- **Platform Support**: Ensure that the stack supports the platforms you want to target, including **mobile** (Android, iOS), **desktop** (Windows, macOS, Linux), and **web**.
- **Community & Support**: A strong, active community and good documentation are critical when facing challenges during development.
- **Future Scalability**: Choose a stack that will allow you to scale the app as your user base grows.
- **Performance**: Certain tech stacks, like **C# with .NET MAUI** or **C++** (for game development), offer better performance than others.

1.2 Popular Cross-Platform Tech Stacks

Here are some of the most popular and effective tech stacks for cross-platform development, depending on your project's needs:

1.2.1 Python-Based Stack

- **Frontend/UI**: **PyQt, Kivy, Tkinter**
- **Backend: Flask, Django, FastAPI**
- **Mobile: BeeWare, Kivy** (limited mobile support)
- **Database: SQLite, PostgreSQL, MongoDB**
- **Testing**: **pytest, unittest**
- **DevOps: Docker, AWS** (Elastic Beanstalk), **Azure Functions**

Python is perfect for data-heavy apps, backend services, and applications that require rapid development.

1.2.2 C#-Based Stack

- **Frontend/UI**: **.NET MAUI, Xamarin, Avalonia** (for desktop)
- **Backend: ASP.NET Core, Blazor** (for web)
- **Mobile: Xamarin, .NET MAUI**
- **Database: SQL Server, SQLite, MongoDB**
- **Testing: xUnit, NUnit, MSTest**
- **DevOps: Azure DevOps, GitHub Actions, Docker**

C# is ideal for building high-performance, enterprise-grade apps with **native UI** across multiple platforms, particularly for mobile and desktop apps.

1.2.3 JavaScript/TypeScript-Based Stack

- **Frontend/UI**: **React Native** (mobile), **Electron** (desktop), **React.js**, **Vue.js** (web)
- **Backend**: **Node.js, Express.js**
- **Database**: **MongoDB, PostgreSQL, MySQL**
- **Testing**: **Jest, Mocha**
- **DevOps**: **Docker, AWS Lambda, Google Cloud Functions**

This stack is highly suitable for building **web apps** and **mobile apps** with a unified **JavaScript** or **TypeScript** codebase.

2. Best Practices for Structuring Projects

A well-organized project structure is essential to keep the codebase maintainable, testable, and scalable. Below are some best practices for structuring your cross-platform projects:

2.1 Follow a Modular Architecture

Break your application into **modules** or **microservices** so each component can be developed, tested, and deployed independently.

Example Project Structure:

bash

```
/project-root
  /src
    /app
      /models
      /views
      /controllers
    /services
      /auth-service
      /data-service
    /assets
      /images
      /styles
    /tests
      /unit-tests
      /integration-tests
  /docs
  /scripts
  /config
    /local
    /prod
```

```
/build
/dist
```

- **/models**: Contains the data models and logic.
- **/views**: Stores the UI components and screens.
- **/controllers**: Holds the application logic.
- **/services**: Includes business logic, API calls, and background tasks.
- **/tests**: Contains test files for each module or service.

2.2 Use Platform-Specific Folders

For cross-platform applications, it's a good idea to have platform-specific folders for **custom code, UI components**, or **performance optimizations** unique to a particular platform.

Example:

bash

```
/project-root
  /src
    /platforms
      /android
      /ios
      /windows
```

```
/macos
```

- Store platform-specific configuration and code in these folders to separate concerns while keeping the rest of the codebase **unified**.

2.3 Implement Continuous Integration/Continuous Deployment (CI/CD)

Set up **CI/CD pipelines** to automate testing, building, and deployment processes, ensuring your application works seamlessly across all platforms.

- **CI tools** like **GitHub Actions**, **Jenkins**, and **Azure DevOps** allow you to automate the entire development lifecycle.
- Make sure your pipeline tests the application on multiple platforms (Windows, macOS, Linux) before deploying.

2.4 Follow Cross-Platform UI Guidelines

253

While it's essential to have a consistent experience across platforms, each platform has its own **design guidelines**. Here are a few tips:

- Use **.NET MAUI** for C# apps to achieve **native UIs** across mobile and desktop platforms.
- In **Python**, use **PyQt** or **Kivy** for developing **native-feel desktop apps**.
- For **mobile apps**, consider frameworks like **React Native** or **Flutter** to maintain **consistent designs** while respecting platform-specific conventions.

3. Final Tips & Resources for Continuous Learning

3.1 Final Tips for Building Cross-Platform Projects

- **Start Small**: Begin with a simple prototype or MVP (minimum viable product) to understand your tech stack and how it works across platforms.
- **Test Frequently**: Cross-platform apps require **continuous testing** on each target platform. Implement automated tests to verify platform-specific behaviors.
- **Leverage Cloud Services**: Use cloud services for **authentication, database management**, and **push**

notifications across platforms to minimize code duplication.

- **Focus on Performance**: Optimize your app to ensure that it runs smoothly across all platforms, especially when dealing with resource-heavy tasks like rendering or processing data.

3.2 Resources for Continuous Learning

- **Python Documentation**: Official Python docs are an excellent resource for learning best practices and new features.
  Python Docs

- **C# Documentation**: Microsoft's C# documentation and **.NET Core** resources offer in-depth guides for cross-platform   development.
  C# Docs

- **Microsoft Learn**: Great for learning **.NET MAUI** and other Microsoft technologies for cross-platform app development.
  Microsoft Learn

- **MDN Web Docs**: Learn about **Progressive Web Apps (PWAs)** and other web technologies.
  MDN Web Docs

255

- **YouTube Channels**: Channels like **Traversy Media**, **The Net Ninja**, and **Academind** provide tutorials on modern cross-platform frameworks like **Flutter**, **React Native**, and **.NET MAUI**.

3.3 Online Communities for Support

- **Stack Overflow**: Ask and answer technical questions about cross-platform development.
- **Reddit**: Subreddits like **r/learnpython**, **r/dotnet**, and **r/crossplatform** offer a lot of support for developers.
- **GitHub**: Explore **open-source projects** to learn from others and contribute to cross-platform projects.

What's Next?

You're now equipped with the knowledge to start building your own **cross-platform applications**. Whether you're creating a mobile app, a desktop app, or a cloud-based solution, the possibilities are vast. Keep experimenting, keep learning, and build software that reaches users across every platform!

www.ingramcontent.com/pod-product-compliance
Lightning Source LLC
LaVergne TN
LVHW051443050326
832903LV00030BD/3208